BEST JOKES FROM TALK RADIO

jokes by category to warm any audience
(and clever riddles to stump your favorite wiseguy)

By popular talk show host
DR. BILL WATTENBURG
(Author of the hilarious bestselling satire How To Find And
Fascinate A Mistress--and survive in spite of it all)

A copy of this book may be ordered by sending a check or money order
for $10 00 plus $2.50 for postage and handling to:

Montgomery Street Press
P.O. Box 810
Chico, CA 95927-0810

(It is usually more convenient and less expensive to have your
bookseller order this book for you by using ISBN 0-913136-10-7)

ISBN 0-913136-10-7

First printing July 1993

Second printing November 1993

Editing and layout by Diane Reilly

Cover design by Tanya Lynn Wattenburg

Printed by Consolidated Printers, Inc.

Berkeley, California

JOKES

RIDDLES

INTRODUCTION

For the past twenty years, I've had the privilege of hosting a late-night, free-for-all, radio talk show called "The Open Line To The West Coast" over ABC station KGO RADIO 810AM, San Francisco, Saturday and Sunday nights from 10pm to 1am. This show has held the top ratings in the market for the last ten years -- which is clearly due to the delightful people who call my show from all over the Pacific Coast of the North American continent. They know they can say whatever they want. I have no idea what the subject of the next call will be. The arguments are usually intense. But the humor has been outrageous -- and often appropriately stinging for us pompous souls who think we know it all.

There is one thing I have learned for certain: Anytime you offer clever minds an opportunity to address millions of listeners -- and yet remain anonymous -- you are tapping directly into an untold wealth of native humor and clever satire.

If you tell folks that they can say what's on their minds on a talk radio show, you have to live with the consequences. The peoples' satire and ribald jokes sometimes disturb one overly-sensitive group or another, as you'll read in this book. Soon, however, along comes turn-about-is-fair-play and it all seems to balance out before the end of the show. But, you can bet that I have been called into the station manager's office more than once and stood there humbly apologetic, dusting off my trousers with my baseball cap, while piles of letters from offended listeners are shoved in my face.

The working people -- farmers, truck drivers, housewives, cowboys -- invariably come up with the most hilarious satire on the foolishness of our times, as you will see. Invariably, the real shockers I've heard on the air have come from women. Women, at least those in my audience, seem to have that exquisite sense of when some subject has been stretched too far, or when other callers are reaching way over their heads. Then the clever housewife calls and delivers a choice bit of satire that paints us foolish. More than a few women have taken me down a notch or two on the air, as you'll read in PUT DOWNS FOR MEN and THE MISSING DOLLAR riddle.

I've attempted to list the jokes by the subject that was being discussed on talk radio when the humor arrived. This may give the reader a better appreciation of what motivated the humor or stinging satire before it blossomed on the air-- or suggest the appropriate time and place to pass on the story in the future. The stories are recorded here in much the same way they were presented live to the talk radio audience.

I've added some of my favorite party riddles at the end. I think you will find, as I have on the air, that one or more of these will tame your favorite smartass when he or she is showing off just a little bit too much -- as you will see in SPINNING QUARTER ON THE BAR. If you would like to discover that you--or your kids--may be just as smart as your favorite Ph.D., try the THIRTEEN CARDS IN ORDER puzzle, my all-time favorite.

MEDICAL MYSTERIES

1. The subject on my talk show to the west coast one night was "advances in medical science". The expert guest in the studio was a professor of medicine who was fascinating the audience with his claims that modern medical science could now correctly diagnose almost any disease of the human body. My guest dispensed two hours of free medical advice to appreciative callers who had obtained no satisfaction from their own doctors. I was barely able to punch up our last caller who had waited patiently on long distance from Arizona. He offered a medical mystery that he just knew our very confident doctor would want to remember:

He said a friend of his, Harry Smith, had suffered horrible migraine headaches all his life. Harry had spent a fortune seeking a cure at dozens of our best medical centers, to no avail. The constant pain was so bad that Harry was seriously considering suicide. Then a friend told Harry about the amazing successes of a medical group in Tel Aviv. With nothing to lose, Harry used the last of his life savings to buy a ticket to Israel.

After five days of exhaustive testing and examination, a team of the best Israeli doctors informed Harry that they had discovered his problem. His testicles were overproducing the hormone testosterone. This was over stimulating his nervous system and giving him the migraine headaches. There were two possible cures: One, he could take anti-testosterone pills the rest of his life; or, two, he could submit to castration and be free of the problem for life. There was no question in Harry's mind. He would not take pills the rest of his life. "Do the surgery as quickly as you can", he commanded.

The morning after surgery, Harry woke up in his hospital bed to the first day of his adult life without a killing headache. He was absolutely overjoyed. It was a beautiful spring day and he could actually hear the birds chirping outside the window without it sounding like a jackhammer on his brain. He jumped out of bed, grabbed his clothes, and raced out of the hospital to greet the beautiful world he had never been able to enjoy.

He was hobbling down a narrow street lined with small stores when he spotted a haberdasher's shop. Impulsively, he stepped in and announced that he wanted a whole new wardrobe for the new life he was about to begin.

Eventually, the haberdasher was measuring him for undershorts. The old craftsman called out to his assistant in the back room: "36".

Harry interrupted him quickly with, "No, no, sir, I always wear size 34."

Down on his knees, the old tailor patiently applied the measuring tape to Harry again. And again, he called out to his waiting assistant, "36".

"No, no, I always wear 34," Harry protested vigorously.

With a deep sigh that called on the wisdom of the ages, the old haberdasher shoved his reading glasses high up on his balding forehead and scowled at his difficult customer. "Mister, I tell you something. Already have I saved hundreds like you from hospital. You wear shorts too tight, pinch testicles, give you tremendous headache."

2.   At another time, a physician guest on my show fielded a question from a woman caller about the medical affliction known as priapus, or "prolonged and painful erection". With a straight face and a serious tone, our doctor in the studio carefully explained that this affliction was no laughing matter to middle-aged or older men who suffered the problem. It was often caused by a blockage in the blood circulation in the penis which would not allow release of the blood pressure in this delicate

organ.   Untreated, he explained, this affliction could lead to serious infection -- or even amputation in the worst cases.

"I know," said the lady on the telephone.   "My husband sometimes has this problem.   He was seeing a doctor, but he would never take his medication properly.   One Saturday night he woke up at midnight with a painful erection and it would not go away -- even though we worked on it for hours," she chuckled. "And he couldn't contact his doctor."

"So, what happened?" asked our medical expert.

"Well," she continued, "he finally put on his raincoat and drove to an all-night drugstore.   But then he saw a woman behind the pharmacy counter.   He asked her if there was anyone else available.   She said there was only her sister in the back room. He started to leave, but she told him that she was a professional pharmacist and that he shouldn't be embarrassed to tell her his problem."

"So," she continued with a laugh, "my poor husband flipped open his raincoat and showed her the problem.   In great embarrassment, he explained that we had done everything we could to relieve the problem at home and that he couldn't contact his doctor.   He simply asked the lady pharmacist: 'What can you give me for this?' "

"My husband told me that the startled pharmacist scratched her head and said she would have to consult with her older sister in the back room.   Ten minutes later, she came back with maybe the best answer I've ever heard for this terrible problem.   She said: 'Mister, this late at night, the best we can do is $10,000 and half the business.' "

(While my studio staff quickly cupped their mouths and gagged in uncontrollable laughter, I kicked myself for not adding the best comment I've ever heard on this subject.   It came from Dirty Harry himself while we were shooting the movie "The Dead

Pool" in 1988. Someone mentioned the subject of priapus and Eastwood, with typical wry wit, commented: "I've got a urologist friend who has a sign in his waiting room for troubled patients. It reads: NEVER FEAR. PRIAPUS CAN BE LICKED.")

3.   A doctor called my show to tell me about one of the strangest cases he had ever encountered. A man walked into his office and said that he could not control the urge to break wind when he was in public. "Doc, it's terrible. Right in the middle of all my friends, I let go. I can't help it. They don't smell or anything, but they're so loud I'm embarrassed to death."

The doctor told him to undress for an examination of his posterior. Just as the doc was examining his rectal area, the guy cut loose right in the doc's face. The patient spun around and exclaimed: "See what I told you, they don't smell or anything, but, God, are they loud and embarrassing."

The doc said, "Hmmm," and walked to a cabinet where he pulled out a frightening instrument that looked like a drill big enough to bore out a stove pipe.

The patient exclaimed: "Good Lord, Doc! You're not going to use that on my ass, are you?"

The doctor waved the drill at him and responded: "No, son, I'm going to use it on your nose -- so you can smell."

4.   A few minutes later, another doctor called to make his contribution to the professional humor of the hour:

It was a hot, sultry day in New York. A tired stockbroker decided to stop in a local bar for a quick drink before he caught his train home to Long Island. Behind the bar, a one-eyed bartender had just been fitted for a new glass eye. He was having trouble keeping the glass eye in place.

The stockbroker ordered a martini on the rocks. The bartender leaned over behind the bar to scoop some ice into the glass after he had poured the gin. His glass eye fell out into the drink. He was too embarrassed to fish it out in front of his customer. He thought, " What the hell? I'll get it out after the guy leaves".

But this customer was dying of thirst. He swallowed the drink, ice cubes, glass eye, and all, and raced out to catch his train.

Two days later, the stockbroker was in mortal pain with constipation, not realizing that the glass eye was lodged firmly in his colon. He walked into a medical building and found the name of a doctor who specialized in intestinal problems. The doctor suggested a thorough examination.

The patient was bent over as the doctor viewed the inside of his colon with a special scope. Suddenly, the doctor jerked out the instrument, stood up to face his patient, and announced indignantly: "Look, mister, if you don't trust me, you can find yourself another doctor down the hall."

5.   An intern at San Francisco General Hospital called my show to tell us a story that was circulating about Doogy Houser, the teenage doctor on television. Doogy was in the examining room with a naive young lady who was troubled about the bumps that were appearing on her chest.

"Don't worry about that," said Doogy. "Your breasts are beginning to develop. It's a natural part of maturing into a woman."

"Yes, but doctor, I'm getting this ugly hair under my arms as well," she said.

"That's just part of the same maturation process," said Doogy very professionally, as he turned to see the next patient.

The girl pulled down her pants to her knees and summoned him back. "But, look! I'm even getting hair down here."

Frustrated to make her understand, Doogy pulled down the front of his pants and responded: "See, I've got the same thing. All grown-ups have hair in the pubic area. It's very natural."

The girl's eyes widened at her first sight of a naked man. "Oh, when do I get one of those?" she giggled.

Young Doogy sighed and said: "Just as soon as I can lock this damn door."

6.   The last medical story that night came from a researcher at the U.C. Medical Center who informed my radio audience that a much publicized research project to use processed chicken blood as a substitute for human blood had been cancelled. Naturally, I asked why.

His answer: "Well, things were going very well, as you probably read in the papers. We had twenty college student volunteers who suffered no ill effects after being transfused with our new chicken blood substitute. We were ready to put this life-saving development on the market. But then, in our follow-up of the group, we discovered that the boys were becoming very cocky and the girls were laying better...

COWBOYS

1.   The manager of a small town bank noticed that every morning a cowboy came into his bank and deposited large sums of cash. The manager decided that he should meet this very important customer. He approached the cowboy, introduced himself, and politely inquired: "What kind of business are you in, Mr Smith?"

The cowboy answered, "I make bets."

"What kind of bets might that be, Mr. Smith?"

"Well, for instance, I'll bet you $10,000 that you have only one testicle, Mr. Bank Manager,"   the cowboy said in all seriousness.

The disbelieving bank manager quickly responded, "Hey, I'll take that bet anytime."

"OK," said the cowboy. "I'll be back at ten tomorrow morning and we'll check you out."

At ten the next morning, the cowboy entered the bank with a well-dressed New York stockbroker right behind him.   He motioned for the bank manager to follow the two of them into the men's room.   There, the bank manager gingerly dropped his trousers. The cowboy reached down to check him out.

"Guess you got two testicles," groused the cowboy gambler. "You win. Here's your $10,000."

Suddenly, the curious stockbroker standing behind them fainted and collapsed to the floor.

"What's wrong with him?" asked the delighted bank manager.

"Oh, don't mind him," answered the cool cowboy. "He's just a smart-ass stockbroker. I bet him $50,000 that I could have a bank manager by the balls by noon today."

2.   Several cowboys from thoughout the west coast called my show one night to cry their woes about how difficult life on the ranch had become for the old-time cowpoke these days. I listened patiently to their hard luck stories for almost a half hour. Then a lady with a real country western accent called and asked me the blunt question: "Bill, you've been listening to those poor cowboys all night. Do you know what the rodeo position is?"

"Well, I've heard of the missionary position, but I've never heard of the rodeo position," I chuckled.

So she proceeded to give me this story:

A raunchy cowboy and his wife had been fighting for years because of his drinking and chasing wild women in the local bars. In a drunken stupor one night, he drove his car off the road and was hospitalized near death for several months. Once back on his feet, he got religion and repented his sins. He and his wife asked the local preacher how to patch up their marriage. The preacher told them that they should confess all their sins to each other and begin a new life based on absolute honesty.

That night they were making love in bed. The wife was overcome with the urge to confess something. "My love," she whispered in his ear as she pulled his head close to hers, "before we were married I was also dating your best friend, Jack, once in a while. I didn't know which one of you I liked the best. But, I'm happy I married you."

Her cowboy husband likewise whispered in her ear: "Sweety, I have to confess something too. Before I went to the hospital, I was having an affair with your best friend, Suzy, next door."

That was the end of her story. I waited a moment for the punch line and then asked: "What's this have to do with the rodeo position you were going to tell us about?"

With the voice of bitter experience, she answered: "Bill dear, the rodeo position is when that cheating cowboy tries to stay in the saddle for the next ten seconds."

The following stories all came from the same good ol' cowboy somewhere out in northern Nevada. He kept my audience chuckling for a week as he treated us each night to one of his hard luck stories from the old west.

3.   A cowboy down on his luck took a part-time job as a gardener for the richest family in town. One afternoon, the matron of the house invited him to lay down his shovel and have some cookies and coffee she had prepared for him in the kitchen. She then took him on a tour of the house. They ended up in the bedroom.

As they were making love, she suddenly grabbed his shoulders to stop his motion and said: "Shhh. I hear someone coming."

The startled cowboy raised up on his elbows, stared at her incredulously, and said: "My, you have good ears, Mame."

4.   At his next job, he was smooching with the lady of the house on the couch in her front room when she blurted out: "Oh my God, my husband is here."

The cowboy calmly asked her: "You have a back door here?"

"No," she answered frantically.

"Well, where do you want one, Mame?"

5. This poor cowboy was finally down on his luck and had to seek food and shelter at the local church mission. A hot meal of beef stew and corn bread was available to those who attended the revival meeting each evening. The cowboy picked up his bowl of stew and corn bread and sat down next to an old wino in a back row of the tent. The preacher was calling the converts forward to be saved at the altar.

One tearful lady in a short, tight skirt, low-cut top, and red high heels was overcome by the sermon. She staggered forward and cried out to the heavens: "Preacher, I've sleep in the arms of drunken cowboys, I've slept in the arms of horny sailors, but now I'm in the arms of the Lord."

The toothless old wino, who had been gumming his corn bread soaked in stew juice while taking in the sights, sat down his bowl, rose to his feet, and shouted his approval: "Atta girl, Sweety, get 'em all while you're at it."

6. The cowboy finally got a job in the big city of Reno. He took his first paycheck and went looking for a car. At one dealership he spotted a cherry of a 1937 Ford coupe. But there was a gorgeous blond sitting behind the wheel as if she were ready to drive it away. Curious, the cowboy asked the salesman the price on the '37 Ford.

"Twenty-five hundred dollars," snapped the salesman.

"You got to be kidding," said the cowboy. "A car that old isn't worth a nickel over three hundred dollars."

"You see that blond behind the wheel?"

"Yah," answered the cowboy. "So what?"

"Well, she goes with the car," said the salesman.

"Now, that's different," said the cowboy. "I'll take it."

The cowboy wheeled his fine car out on the freeway with the blond sitting quietly beside him. He turned off on the first dirt road he saw. He stopped and slid across the seat to put his arm around the blond. "How about a little, Sweety?" he smiled.

The blond pulled away shaking her head and said: "Sorry, Sonny, you got that when you paid twenty-five hundred dollars for this old Ford."

7. Our Nevada story-teller left us with one last quicky at the end of the week.

He asked me, "Bill, do you all know the difference between a dog and a fox in a cowboy bar?"

"No," I chuckled, anticipating another bit of his salty wisdom.

"Any tired cowboy just off the cattle drive can tell you that one," he drawled. "The difference is about four whiskeys at the other end of the bar."

8. A Utah cowboy was on his first vacation to San Francisco. He stopped in at the famous Marina Safeway to stock up on food for his camper truck. On his way out, he noticed a well-dressed lady struggling with three large bags of groceries. He gallantly offered to help her carry them out to her car. The San Francisco socialite was a bit suspicious that he might be a con man. She studied the strapping young cowboy for a moment and then smiled her acceptance.

Outside, the glamorous lady stopped to scan the enormous parking lot. The cowboy holding her groceries waited patiently beside her, thinking to himself that this lady was just like his mom back home -- she couldn't remember where she parked her car.

The lady checked her watch and looked over her shoulder to see who might be looking. Then she nudged close to him, stood up on her tiptoes, and whispered tenderly in his ear:

"I have an itchy pussy, big boy. Have any ideas how we might solve the problem?"

The cowboy gave her a bewildered smile and answered: "Darn if I know, Mame. All them damn little Japanese cars look alike to me."

9.   When this bewildered cowboy got back to his small town in Utah, he discovered that the town now had its first doctor in fifty years. A lady doctor who was fresh out of medical school, and a darn good-looker at that.

The cowboy was in the doctor's waiting room the next morning, bursting at the seams to tell his friends about all his strange experiences while he was on vacation in San Francisco.

The nurse finally led him into the examining room. The doctor approached and asked him what his problem was.

"It's my penis, Mame," he mumbled in embarrassment.

"Well, let's have a look," she said very calmly. She popped the buttons on his bib overalls and stripped him down to his shorts. Then, she examined his genitals very professionally. "I don't see a problem here," she reported.

The cowboy beamed a prideful smile and said: "I know, Mame. But ain't it a lulu?"

TEXANS

1.   A Texas businessman was entertaining a New York stockbroker at a barbeque at the Texan's ranch. Naturally, they were trading tall stories about their exploits. Both had a little too much beer to drink and had to relieve themselves. The Texan led his guest away from the party and toward a large swimming pool behind the house. "We never swim in this damn thing. This is all we ever use it for," he bragged.

As they stood on the edge of the pool and held their aim into the water below, the stockbroker thought of a pun of his own. "Hey, that water's cold," he announced.

Not to be undone by a silly New Yorker, the Texan responded: "Yah, and it's deep too, ain't it?"

2.   A truck driver was hauling a load of twenty penguins from Alaska to the San Diego Zoo in a refrigerated trailer when his truck broke down near Bakersfield, California. Under the hot summer sun, the temperature was rising in the trailer. The truck driver was trying to wave down passing cars for help when a Texan in a Cadillac convertible pulled up.

The truck driver pleaded with him, "Mister, I got to get these little penguins to the San Diego Zoo by five o'clock tonight or I'm in a heap of trouble. The poor little devils will die out in this hot sun."

"No problem," said the Texan.   "I'll give 'em a ride down there in nothin' flat. The Texan loaded the penguins into his Cadillac convertible and raced off with the happy little penguins clapping their flippers goodbye to the much relieved truck driver.

Shortly, the driver fixed his truck and headed down the freeway as well. In San Diego, he was driving down the street leading to the zoo, when he spotted the Texan walking toward a movie theater -- with twenty little penguins waddling happily behind him on the sidewalk. The truck driver pulled up alongside them and hollared out at the Texan: "Hey, I thought I told you to take them penguins to the zoo."

The happy Texan beamed a big smile and answered: "Well shucks, I did like you asked, partner. The little buggers had so much fun at the zoo, I thought I'd treat 'em to a movie too.

3. A proud Texan heard that the new state of Alaska was bigger than Texas. He decided that he had to find out if their men could live up to the standards of Texas men. When he arrived in Anchorage, he headed straight for the nearest bar. He cornered the bartender and demanded: "Tell me what it is you have to do to prove you're a man in Alaska?"

The wily bartender answered: "Well, fellow, first you have to drink a quart of this Northern Lights Whiskey. Then, you have to wrestle one of them polar bears out there on the icebergs. And finally, you have to make love to one of our bar girls on the snow when it's twenty below zero outside."

The Texan said: "Gimmie that bottle." He chug-a-lugged the quart of whiskey and asked the bartender to point out a polar bear. The bartender showed him one sitting on a sheet of ice still connected to the shore. The Texan headed for the polar bear.

An hour later, the patrons in the bar heard someone groaning at the front door. The bartender opened the door to find the Texan slowly crawling up the steps on all fours. His back was ripped to shreds and blood was pouring out of the claw marks visible through his torn shirt. The badly injured Texan, nevertheless, looked up at the bartender with a big silly grin on his face and asked in a drunken slur: "Now, where's that bar girl I'm supposed to wrestle?"

4.   A Texas ranch owner decided to visit an old college buddy of his who lived on a small farm in Oklahoma. They hadn't seen each other for twenty years. All was going well with the visit. The Texan was being especially careful not to embarrass his friend over the small size of his Oklahoma farm, but the Texan just had to find a way to brag about his Texas ranch.

They were sitting on the porch one night when the Texan thought of a polite way to make a comparison. "You know," he said, "it takes me all day just to drive around my ranch in Texas in my pickup truck."

The Oklahoma boy took a puff on his pipe, rocked back in his chair, and sympathized with his less fortunate friend:

"Yah, well I remember how it was during hard times. I had a pickup like that once myself."

FARMERS

1.   A reporter heard about a ninety-year-old farmer and his eighty-year-old wife who just had their twelfth baby. He rushed out to the farm to interview them. He found the happy old farmer sitting in his rocking chair with the new baby in his lap and six other little kids pestering him.

"Mister Jones," can you tell me your secret that lets you and your wife still make babies at your age?" asks the disbelieving reporter.

With a sly grin on his face, the old farmer says: "It's like this, boy. Ma gets this here gleam in her eyes and I knows that it's time for us to head for the bedroom, so I goes into the bathroom and gets the vaseline..." The reporter interrupts him.

"Vaseline! What do you need that for?"   asks the naive reporter.

"Well, hell fire sonny, you put it on the doorknob -- to keep these little rascals out."

2.   Ma and Pa Smith bought a new rooster from the mail order catalogue to service the hens in their chicken coop because their old rooster was getting tired. The young rooster jumped out of the box and immediately surveyed all the hens he would soon be serving. Then he encountered the old rooster who said: "I see you're going to be taking over my job. I'd kind'a like to go out with a little pride, if you don't mind. How about racing around the farm house and whoever comes in first will be the head rooster here? That way, at least all the ladies here will know that I didn't just give up without a fight."

The impatient young rooster said: "Sure, pop. Anything you want. But let's be quick about it. I got a lot of work to do here."

The old rooster politely asked again: "Well how about giving me a little head start so I don't look too bad?"

"Anything you want, pop. But let's get going."

The old rooster took off and the young rooster gave him a twenty yard head start. The young rooster poured on the speed to catch up with the old rooster just as they were coming around the farm house in full view of Ma and Pa sitting on the front porch. Pa reached over for his shotgun, took aim, and blasted the young rooster into a ball of feathers. Then he turned to Ma and said: "Ma, we got to call them mail order people. That's the third gay rooster they sent us this month."

3.   Ma began complaining that Pa was slowing down in his sex life, so Pa went to see the local doctor. The doctor gave him some pep pills that were supposed to spike up his sexual urges.

A few weeks later, the doctor stopped by the farmhouse on his rounds. He found Pa sitting on the front porch, obviously sad and dejected. There was a funeral wreath on the front door. "Were's Ma?" asked the doctor.

"She died," answered Pa. "It was them pills you gave me."

"Those pills couldn't have hurt Ma," answered the doctor.

"Oh yeh," said Pa, shaking his head in protest. "That's what you think. The first week I took those pills, I was out on the tractor in the field all day. I would get the urge and go running for the house. But, by the time I got to the bedroom, I was plumb tuckered out. So Ma, the genius she was, suggested that I carry my shot gun with me on the tractor. She told me to fire the shotgun whenever I got the urge and she would come running to meet me half way in the field.

Doc, I'm here to tell you that we was like a couple of teenagers making love in the field every day -- until them damn fools opened duck season and them hunters came along firing their shotguns. She just plumb run her poor self to death."

4. A Wall Street brokerage house bought a Wyoming cattle ranch on a leveraged buy-out. Typically, the first year's profits were nothing compared to what they had expected. They decided to send in an efficiency expert from Harvard Business School to streamline the operation.

The expert set about interviewing all the ranch hands to determine who could be cut from the payroll. Eventually, he came upon an old boy sitting on the rail fence by the pasture. He was slowly sharpening a knife and whistling a western tune while the rest of the hands were running about to look busy.

"And just what is your job here, fellow? asked the efficiency expert, with obvious annoyance in his voice at the sight of this lazy employee.

The old boy held up his knife to look it over as its razor-sharp blade glistened in the sun. He pointed it in the direction of the nosey expert and drawled: "I'm the ranch psychologist here."

The expert thought for a moment and said: "You know, I'm not some dumb cowboy who's never been to town. I think I know what a psychologist does for a living. Now, tell me, if you can, just how you qualify as a ranch psychologist."

With a devilish twinkle in his eyes, the old boy answered: "Easy. See them young bulls over there in the pasture?" The Harvard expert looked off in the distance as the old boy continued: "Well, mister, I'm the guy who takes this here knife and changes their minds from ass to grass."

5. The word got around in the farming community that they now had their first doctor in the county in forty years. A lady doctor had arrived in town with her nurse on one of them government programs that sends doctors into the rural areas, they said. Farmer Jones had been meanin' to see a doctor for months, so he drove into town.

He waited for two hours behind a long line of pregnant women before he was called by the very proper and prim old nurse. "Now tell me your problem, Mr. Jones." she commanded.

"Well, Mame, it's my penis..." he began.

She cut him off immediately with a gasp. "How dare you use such words in front of all these proper ladies! You can just go somewhere else if you can't clean up your language."

Farmer Jones went back to the end of the line and waited another two hours before he was called again. Coldly, the old nurse asked: "Okay. What is your problem this time, Mr. Jones?"

"It's my ear, Mame," he answered sheepishly.

The nurse quickly brightened up and smiled in the direction of the ladies in the waiting room who were nodding their approval.

"Oh, that's so much better, Mr. Jones. So, what's the problem with your ear?"

"I can't piss out of it, Mame."

6. Ma and Pa from Nebraska were taking their first vacation in forty years by driving to Disneyland in California. Ma sat in the back seat all the way and issued a steady stream of orders to poor old Pa. She was so hard of hearing that she never heard the choice remarks that Pa muttered in her direction.

On the outskirts of Los Angeles, they pulled into a service station for gas. Pa had been dreaming about relaxing for a few minutes to read the paper, without Ma's constant commentary.

The station attendant came to the window and asked Pa what he wanted. "Fill'er up," said Pa.

"What'd he say, Pa? What'd he say?" Ma barked from the back seat.

"He asked what we wanted, and I told him to fill it," answered Pa after he put down his paper.

"Okay, Pa. That's Okay," conceded Ma after some thought.

The attendant had to make small talk as he held the nozzle in the tank. "Where you folks from?" he asked Pa.

"We're from Nebraska," answered Pa.
"What'd he say, Pa? What'd he say?" snapped Ma.

Pa put down his paper to turn around once again so Ma could hear him. "He asked where we're from, and I told him we're from Nebraska."

"Okay, Pa. that's Okay," said Ma.

The bored attendant then thought of something relevant. "You know, I was in Nebraska once," he said. "I met a strange lady there who took me to her farm one weekend. That was the worst lay I've ever had in my life. I had to get out of there -- in a hurry," he chuckled.

What'd he say, Pa? What'd he say?" Ma screeched again.

Pa put his paper down for the third time, turned around to look Ma straight in the eye, and said sweetly: "He sez he thinks he know'd you, Ma."

7.   Farmer Smith's wife was turning moody and just downright mean at times. At first he thought it was because he was working long hours during the harvest. However, she was even more grouchy when he was home all day during the winter months. Finally, he decided to take her to the doctor.

Farmer Smith waited outside while the doc had a long talk with his wife. Then he called in farmer Smith. "Mr. Smith, I think the problem with your wife is that we need to figure out how she can get more sex."

Farmer Smith thought this over for a moment and replied: "Well, doc, let's see. I have lodge meetings on Monday and Wednesday nights and we go to Grange meetings on Saturday and church on Sunday. Sooo, let's see," he mused as he flipped the pages of his calendar book. "Yes, it looks like you can have her on Monday, Wednesday, and Friday nights."

8.   Down the road a piece, farmer Jones was not feeling well. He went to the doctor for the first time in forty years. The diagnostic tests showed that he had gall bladder problems. He was scheduled for surgery.

Farmer Jones was not at all happy with the hospital food during his recovery. He complained bitterly about the watery soup they served him with his first no-solids meal. He demanded that the nurse take it away. The nurse tried to explain to him that he couldn't eat heavier foods until he had a bowel movement.

His first bowel movement hadn't arrived by the second day, and he again received a bowl of soup and crackers for lunch. Again he sent it away, with some bitter words to the nurse.

His doctor decided late that night that Mr. Jones should have some medication and an emema to loosen him up a bit. He was sleeping soundly when the nurse arrived with her equipment. She rolled him over and applied the enema as he squirmed in his sleep. By the next day, he was back to normal. He ate his first full meal, and he was scheduled to be released the next morning.

As he was being placed in a wheelchair for his ride down to discharge, they brought his long-time neighbor, farmer Smith, to the hospital room.
"What they got you in here fer, Henry? asked farmer Jones.

"Bad back, George," answered farmer Smith. "Got any suggestions for me on how to survive this place?" he joked.

"Yeh," groused farmer Jones. "Take the soup, or they'll sneak up on ya in the middle of the night and shove it up your ass."

9. A group of Nebraska farmers were sitting around the pot-bellied stove in the general store one winter day. They were swapping stories about the meanest things they had ever done as a practical joke. Farmer Jed began to chuckle when it came his turn to tattle on himself.

"Well, I'll tell ya," Jed laughed. "I was driving by Henry's pumpkin patch last November when I got this terrible urge to go take a crap. There was nowhere to go, so I went over in that there pumpkin patch and I spotted the biggest damn pumpkin I ever saw in these parts. I took my pocket knife and cut the top out, and I dumped right in that pumpkin. Then I set the top back on that big pumpkin so's nobody'd know the difference."

The old boys gathered around the stove roared with laughter -- all except Smitty. He got up, solemn faced, and walked over to the telephone. He cranked the handle to make one long and three short rings. His mother answered on the other end.

"Ma, I got something to confess," Smitty said to his mother who was home cooking his evening meal. "You were right about that pumpkin pie on Thanksgiving."

10.   Jolly old farmer Jones celebrated his ninety-fourth birthday in his wheelchair on the farm surrounded by his family members. When the day was over, he announced that he had finally decided that he would move into the modern rest home they had long recommended in case he needed medical care. His family was sad, but they knew it was best for him.

The nurses at the rest home were delighted over his general good health at his age, with one exception. He had a strange affliction. Several times a day his whole body would suddenly jerk and he would lean way over to the left as he slumbered in his wheelchair. They consulted the house doctor who concluded that the old man suffered from a mild form of epilepsy. The doctor prescribed medication which they began giving him with his meals.

However, the nurses were afraid that he would fall out of his wheelchair and hurt himself.   They kept a close eye on him. Each time he suffered a seizure they would rush over to set him up straight in his chair and hold him until he was stable.

His family came to visit him on the first weekend of his stay. "Grandpa, how are they treating you?" one granddaughter cheerfully asked.

Grandpa gave them a frown of unhappiness and responded with a bit of annoyance in his voice:

"Well, the food's OK. The room is comfortable, I guess. But, you know, these people won't let a man fart."

LITTLE KIDS

1.   A twelve-year-old farm boy decided to run away from home. He had no trouble hitch-hiking to the big city, but there he discovered that he would have to find a job if he wanted to eat. He wandered into a drugstore and confidently asked the druggist for a job. It just happened that the the druggist needed someone to watch the store because he had to run to the bank. So, he sat the kid behind the cash register and told him: "Don't do a thing, don't sell a thing while I'm gone. Tell the customers I'll be back in ten minutes."

Shortly after the druggist left, a man came into the store with a horrible case of whooping cough. He was coughing his head off, and he begged the kid to help him. The kid looked up on the shelf and saw some bottles labled "crotin oil" (which in those parts was the name for an extreme laxative used by farmers. One teaspoon will empty the insides of any animal in ten minutes -- out both ends.)

The kid's eyes sparkled with a bright idea. He handed a bottle to the poor devil in front of him and proudly announced: "That'll be a dollar, mister."

A few minutes later, the druggist returned and jokingly asked, "Make any big sales while I was gone?"

The kid answered very proudly, "Well, I sold a bottle of this stuff to a man with the whooping cough," as he pointed up to the crotin oil.

"Good lord, boy!" exclaimed the druggist. "That won't cure the whooping cough."

"Oh no," said the kid, as he pointed out the window. "You see that feller out there leaning up against the telephone pole?"

"So what about him?" asked the druggist.

With a knowing grin, the kid said: "He's afraid to cough."

2.   A mail-order insurance salesman called my talk show to tell me what happened to him once when he was making cold calls to homeowners to drum up new business:

A little boy answered the phone. He spoke in a very nervous whisper. The salesman said: "I can barely hear you. Is your mommy home?"

The little boy whispered fearfully, "Yes, but she can't come to the phone."

"Well, is your daddy home?"

"Yes," whispered the little boy again, with his hand cupped over his mouth, "but he can't come to the phone either."

"Is anyone else there?" demanded the persistent salesman.

"The whisper answered, hesitantly, "Yes, there's a policeman here."

"Can he come to the phone?"

"No," whispered the boy.

"Well, is there anyone besides the policeman?"

"Yes, there is a fireman here."

"Put him on the phone then, little boy," demanded the salesman, suspecting that the boy was in some danger.

"He can't come either," whispered the boy.

"Little boy, what the hell is going on there?" demanded the worried salesman. "Your mommy and daddy can't come to the phone. There's a policeman and a fireman there, and they can't come to the phone. Are they looking for someone?"

"Yes," whispered the boy, after a long pause.

"Ah," said the salesman, relieved that he was finally getting somewhere. "WHO are they looking for?"

"Me," whispered the little boy.

3.   A very bright farm boy who lived on an isolated cattle ranch in Lyons County, Nevada, was allowed to roam around a small Nevada town for the first time one Saturday afternoon while his dad shopped for supplies at the local general store. It didn't take him long to discover that there was one particular house in town that was very popular with all the ranch hands who were in town for the weekend to spend their paychecks. The boy was fascinated as he watched the colorful madam greet the cowboys at the front door. He sat across the street and watched the men come and go.

Meanwhile, inside, a drunken, horny cowboy kicked off his boots and Levis as soon as he entered a working lady's second-story bedroom. He raced like a madman to make contact with her as soon as she had disrobed. The momentum of his charge thrust the two of them out the front window. The couple fell the short distance to the wooden sidewalk below, still locked together in a sexual embrace. Realizing that she was unhurt, the naked lady broke into hilarious laughter as the cowboy did his thing.

The boy observed this absurd scene from across the street for a moment. Then he calmly stepped around the bouncing couple and knocked on the cathouse door. The madam opened the door and immediately scolded the boy for encroaching on territory clearly forbidden to youngsters. The boy held up his hands defensively to signal that he didn't want to go in. He just had something to tell her.

With a genuine worried look on his innocent face, he announced: "Mame, I just thought that someone should tell you that your sign fell down."

4. Twelve-year-old Johnny's mother forced him to attend a piano recital by his ten-year-old cousin, Jeffery. Johnny despised his snotty cousin who was too good to play Little League with the rest of the boys. He might dirty his fingernails.

At the recital, poor Jeffery was extremely nervous as he faced the crowd of smiling relatives who had been assembled by his mother. In the middle of the first piece he played, he had the overwhelming urge to fart. He knew he couldn't hold it for long, so he pounded the keys furiously to cover the noise and then he let go. However, the loud rip was heard by all. His poor mother turned red with embarrassment.

But cousin Johnny saved the day. From the audience, he barked out: "Fido, get out from under the piano!"

Everyone suddenly noticed Jeffery's dog under the piano stool. Jeffery, in particular, sighed relief that the dog was being blamed for his indiscretion.

Shortly, the budding artist Jeffery was again seized by the same urge as he struggled through his second piano concerto. He quickly glanced down to see that his dog was still under the piano stool. The dog was there. Jeffery let go another rumbling rip that could be heard over a freight train.

Thoroughly bored, Johnny rose to his feet again. His mother beside him swelled with pride that her son would once more save the day and relieve his talented cousin of this public shame. Like an admiral under fire, Johnny pointed at the dog and shouted:

"Fido, if you don't get out of there, he's going to shit on you the next time."

5.   Tommy the Terror, as he was known to his teachers in school, was riding down the street in his wagon being pulled by his pet goat when he met little Mary from his third-grade class. "Whoa doat. Dit in, girl," he commanded. Little Mary got in the wagon. "Dit up doat," he ordered.

Quickly, he asked Mary to take off her dress. Mary refused.

"Dit out, girl," he growled. "Dit up doat."

Then he saw Suzy. "Whoa doat. Dit in girl," he commanded again. And little Suzy got in the wagon. "Dit up doat, he ordered.

Suzy likewise refused his advances. Tommy again barked: "Whoa doat. Dit out girl. Dit up doat."

When little Kathy refused him as well, his frustration surfaced in his final orders: "Whoa doat. Dit out girl. Dit in doat."

6.   The carnival came to town with a new animal show to relieve the small-town suckers of their money. An old elephant stood in a tent with a sign painted on his side. It said:

"Make this elephant jump off of all four feet, and you win a hundred dollars. No firearms or loud noises allowed."

Little Johnny took one look at this and went running to find his mother. He borrowed a hat pin from her and returned to the tent. He paid his dollar to the gate keeper and approached the elephant.

First, he caught the elephant's eye and waved the sharp hat pin for the sleepy-eyed animal to see. The gate keeper watched with amusement as the silly kid then put on a familiar show for the thoroughly bored elephant. Johnny pretended to jab himself in the butt with the sharp needle as he playfully jumped off both feet to instruct the stoic elephant.

These fools all think that elephant is going to play follow-the-leader, the gate keeper thought to himself as he turned away to greet the next sucker with money to lose. Just then, Johnny walked behind the elephant and jabbed him in the testicles with the hat pin. The elephant let out a huge roar and leaped off of all four feet. The crowd applauded their approval.

The gate keeper was furious. Reluctantly, he paid the hundred dollars -- and then promptly added another exclusion to the sign: "You can't touch the elephant."

The next day, little Johnny was back in line with his dollar. The gate keeper watched him closely as he approached the elephant. When Johnny pulled out the hat pin again, the keeper was on him in an instant. "You can't touch the elephant with that," commanded the keeper.

"No problem," said Johnny. "I just want to say hello to him."

Johnny whispered something in the elephant's ear. The elephant promptly jumped off of all four feet. The keeper was flabergasted. "What in the hell did you say to that elephant?" asked the heartbroken carnival shark as he counted out another hundred dollars for Johnny.

"Oh, I just asked him if I had to jab him in the balls again."

7.   Back at home the next day, little Johnny's mother started down the stairs to the basement in their house to fetch some potatoes she had stored there. As she looked down, she got the shock of her life. There was little Johnny with the neighbor girl, Anne Belle. They had their clothes off and they were playing

man and wife. Their toys were scattered all around them and they were munching graham crackers from an open box on the floor as they played with each other.

Johnny's mother rushed back upstairs and broke into tears. Just then, his father came home. She frantically told him what she had seen and demanded that he do something about it, immediately!

His father contemplated the situation for a moment with a disturbed frown on his face. He peeked down the basement stairs to take a look for himself. Then he took off his coat, turned to the refrigerator, and pulled a steak out of the freezer. He dropped it in a skillet and turned up the gas. His wife hit the ceiling.

"Your ten-year-old son is down there playing with a little girl this very moment, and you're not going to do anything about it!"

"You bet I am," answered her husband emphatically. "My son is not going to screw on graham crackers."

8.   Jimmy Cornhusker, age twelve, decided to run away from the farm where his dad had become totally unreasonable in his demands that Jimmy should milk the cows at least twice a week. He loaded up a backpack with his belongings and walked to the county road to catch a ride to the big city. Soon, a farmer in a brand new nine-passenger Pontiac station wagon picked him up.

Jimmy hopped into the front seat and quickly noticed the spacious seating in the car. "Who thits in that thaht seat way back there?" asked Jimmy.

"I have three little boys that sit back there," answered the farmer.

"Tay, thaht's all right," observed Jimmy with a childish lisp. "But who thits in thaht thecond theat back there?

"I have three little girls who sit there," answered the farmer.

"Thay, thaht's all right. Three little boys and three little girls." Jimmy thought a moment and then asked: "And who thits in this big wide front theat with you, mister?"

"I have a wife and two little babies who sit up here," answered the farmer.

"Thay, thaht's all right. Three little boys, three little girls, and a wife and two babies. Wow!"

Jimmy checked things over again and said: "You know thomthing mister. You almosth th-screwed yourself out of a theat."

9. Two five-year-old boys were playing in the backyard. One of them said:

"Can you guess what I found?"

The other one said: "No, what did you find?"

"I found a condom on the patio this morning."

The other one looked a little puzzled and asked: "What's a patio?"

10. A fifth-grader came home and his mommy asked him what he learned in school that day.

"Oh, we just learned about not getting AIDS."

A bit startled, his mommy asked, apprehensively, "And how do you do that?"

Her preoccupied son took a bite out of his jelly sandwich and mumbled: "Just like I always hear you and daddy talking. "Buy condominiums and don't rush into intersections."

11. It was Christmas time in the local department store. The little kids were lining up at the entrance to sit on Santa's lap and tell him what they wanted for Christmas. But, the store manager was frantic. The professional Santa had called in sick at the last moment. The manager suddenly spotted an old wino who often loitered outside the store. He was about the right size. Why not? However, the manager knew he would smell like the urine-drenched alley behind the store. There was no time to give him a bath.

In a stroke of genius, the manager grabbed a bottle of men's cologne and doused it all over the the old man's body before stuffing him in the Santa costume. The manager was feeling very clever as he led his new, sweet-smelling Santa into the toy department.

Little Mary was first to climb up on Santa's lap. The rudy-faced old wino gave her a big hug and then fixed his bloodshot eyes on her and said: "I know what you want, Sweety." Then he gingerly tapped her on the nose with a shakey finger as he recited the letters, "d-o-l-l, doll."

"Santa, how did you know?" exclaimed little Mary as her mother smiled approvingly nearby.

Suzy was next to jump up on his lap. Santa gave her a bear hug and said: "I know what you want." He tapped her on the nose as he recited the letters, "k-i-t-t-e-n, kitten."

Suzy squeeled with glee as she raced back to her mommy.

The store manager was mentally counting the money he had saved with this dream-come-true Santa Claus.

Meanwhile, little Jimmy, the local Little League Captain, had been watching this silly show with some skepticism as he stood impatiently in line with his mother. She had insisted that he get with the Christmas spirit and talk to Santa before she would buy him any presents. Finally, it was his turn on Santa's lap.

Santa said: "I know what you want, little boy." He tapped Jimmy on the nose as he called out, "t-r-a-i-n, train."

Obviously unimpressed, little Jimmy reached up and tapped Santa on the nose. "And I know what you like, Santa. You like g-i-r-l-s, girls."

"What do you mean by that?" exclaimed the suddenly worried Santa.

Little Jimmy glanced back at his mommy who was glaring at him with a don't-you-dare-say-something-nasty look in her eye. Then he tapped his answer out on Santa's rudy nose:

"Because your finger smells like p-u-..." He paused for a moment as he struggled for the spelling. His mother reached out to gag him. Quickly, Jimmy blurted out the rest of his answer: "...r-f-u-m-e, perfume!"

12. A child psychologist who had heard some of these "little kids" jokes on my radio show finally called with the cutest story I've ever heard:

He said that he specialized in kids who suffered from depression. One of his patients was the son of wealthy parents. The boy often sat alone in his bedroom surrounded by expensive toys that he never touched. One day he asked the boy why he didn't play with his toys.

The boy answered: "Why bother? They're all just going to break anyway."

That afternoon, the psychologist was driving through a run-down area surrounded by farmland. He observed several kids from poor families playing in the dirt. He stopped the car to watch them for a moment. As he looked more closely, he saw one of the boys frantically digging in a pile of horse manure with his bare hands. The boy was throwing the manure in all directions behind him, some of it hitting the other kids nearby.

The psychologist got out of his car and walked up to the boy. He was concerned that this kid was expressing a lot of anger over something.

"Why are you digging in that dirty manure and throwing it all around?" he asked cautiously.

The poor kid dressed in ragged jeans and worn-out tennis shoes stopped his digging for only a moment as he beamed a big smile of anticipation and answered:

"Mister, with all this horse shit piled up here there's got to be a pony in there somewhere for me."

DOGS

1. A child psychologist guest in the studio once treated my talk radio audience to his "Manifesto For Raising a Son". He then launched into a scathing criticism to all the wayward fathers of our materialistic society who were encouraging their sons to be over-achievers. By the pompous tone of his lecture, I just knew there would be a proper response within the next few calls. Sure enough, a truck driver called from a roadside pay phone.

In a slow drawl, he began with:

"Well, I don't have no college degree, but my dad told me a story that has served me well in thirty years of livin' with one good woman and raisin' six kids who ain't never gonna be on welfare."

Here was his story:

A daddy dog decided that it was time to teach his puppy dog the ways of the world. So one morning, puppy dog followed daddy dog out the back door to start his lessons. First thing, daddy dog kicked over the neighbor's garbage can and ate a few items. Puppy dog took that in and thought it was a pretty smart idea. Down the street, they ran into a bitch in heat. Daddy dog prompty accommodated the waiting lady. Puppy dog thought that looked interesting and sensible. Farther down the street, daddy dog spotted a fire plug. He sniffed it over and then raised his hind leg to hose it down. This time, puppy dog was confused.

"Hey, pop, I don't dig this," he said.   First you kick over the garbage can for something to eat. And when you serviced the lady, I kinda understand that. But why are you piss'en on the fire plug?"

The wise old daddy dog answered, "Son, that there's what you gotta do to anything in this world that you can't eat or make love to.

2.   Josh, a hermit swamp rat who lived in the Florida Everglades, came into town one day with his ugly little dog on a barbed-wire leash. He tied his little dog up to the hitching post in front of the general store and marched in to get his supplies for the year. The good ol' boys sunning themselves on the porch called out after him: "Better not leave that there puny little dog out here all alone. We got a mean German shepherd here that will eat him up. He hates strange dogs -- especially ugly little buggers like that'n."

Josh shrugged off the warning: "I reckon he can take care of himself."

"Don't say we never warned ya," chuckled the good ol' boys.

As soon as Josh stepped inside the store, one of the ol' boys got up and unleashed his mean German shepherd.

The big dog leaped off the porch to devour the poor, ugly little mut tied to the hitching post. But the little dog suddenly turned ferocious and ripped the big dog to shreds before his feet ever hit the ground. The little dog was beginning to eat what was left of the prized German shepherd when the swamp rat came out of the store to see the shocked looks on the faces of the good ol' boys.

"What the hell kind'a dog you got there, swamp rat?" they asked in amazement.

The swamp rat smiled through his teeth and answered: "Well, boys, before I bobbed his tail and snipped off his nose, he was an alligator."

3.   Jake Stoolsetter was the owner of the world's only talking dog. He had made an easy living for ten years in the small-town bars of northern Nevada by making bets with disbelieving patrons. First, he would have his dog, Fido, say something

simple in English. Then, he would bet them that Fido could understand any instructions given to him in English.

One guy bet Jake a hundred dollars that his dog couldn't fetch a carton of Marlboro cigarettes from the local grocery store at Fifth and Main Streets. Jake gave Fido the instructions and a twenty dollar bill. Off went Fido.

An hour later, Fido was still not back. Jake had lost his bet, and he was furious. He went looking for his dog. The storekeeper had seen the famous Fido chase another dog behind the grocery store. Jake looked around the corner to discover Fido locked up with a female in heat.

Jake shook his head in disgust and said: "Fido, up until now you have been a perfect dog. You never before did anything like this. Oh, how I trusted you. You really let me down."

Fido looked up from his ridiculous position and answered: "Yah boss. But you never gave me any money before either."

4. Henry was the proud owner of the world's best duck hunting dog. He had taken top honors in every hunting-dog show in the country. But lately, Henry had trained his dog to do something that no dog had ever done. He just had to show this amazing feat to his neighbor, Joe, before he announced it to the world. Joe secretly thought dogs were a pain in the ass. However, he tried to humor Henry whenever he came around to brag about his mut.

Henry dragged Joe out to the duck blind early one morning. A flight of ducks flew over and Henry knocked one down with his shotgun. Then he unleashed his dog and commanded: "Fetch."

Henry's prized dog leaped out of the duck blind and raced across the water to fetch the dead duck. He walked on the water!

The dog's proud owner gave Joe an expectant look. Joe said not a word about the dog walking on water. Perturbed that his neighbor could be so indifferent about this phenomonen, Henry blurted out:

"Joe, for God's sake, didn't you just see something special about my dog?"

Joe thought for a moment and answered with a yawn:

"Yah, Henry, you brought me out here at six in the morning to show me that your thousand-dollar dog can't swim."

TRAINED ANIMALS

1.   Alex had trained his pet octopus to play any musical instrument known to man. He collected a fortune from musicians who would hand the octopus a strange instrument and bet that he couldn't play a particular tune. The octopus succeeded without fail.

Then one day, a Scotsman handed the octopus his bagpipes and bet Alex a thousand dollars that the octopus couldn't play a simple tune on the pipes. The octopus grabbed the bagpipes and began fingering its arms with his tentacles. Soon, he was wrestling with the bagpipes all over the floor, but he couldn't squeeze a tune out of them. The smiling Scotsman collected his money from Alex and his pipes from the frustrated octopus.

Alex scolded his normally faithful octopus: "After all the training I've given you, I can't believe you couldn't play those simple bagpipes."

His octopus looked at him with sorrowful eyes and retorted: "Play her! Hell, I couldn't even get her skirt off."

2.   Grandma Jones was feeling particularly lonely after her grand kids moved away. A church lady told her that she should buy a parrot because they make wonderful pets. Grandma went straight to the pet store on Monday. The pet store owner seized the opportunity to get rid of an old parrot, Dirty Polly they called him, who had picked up every dirty word ever spoken in the store.

Shortly after she put him in his new cage at home, Grandma tickled him under the beak and asked: "Can you speak to me, Polly dear?"

Polly burst out: "Awk, that customer was an asshole."

Grandma was shocked. She grabbed the parrot and stuffed him in the refrigerator for ten minutes to teach him a lesson. Then she put the shivering parrot back in his cage and commanded: "Now maybe you can say something nice."

Polly responded with: "Goddamn! I'm cold."

This time, Grandma grabbed him out of the cage and stuck him in the freezer for twenty minutes. He was almost frozen stiff when she put him back in his cage. When the parrot thawed out, Grandma glared at him and challenged: "I hope that taught you to clean up your language."

Dirty Polly shook his head with a shiver and said: "Awk, what the hell did the turkey say?"

3.   A duck walked into a drugstore and ordered some chapstick.

"Will that be cash or credit card?" asked the druggist.

"Ah, just put it on the bill," said the duck.

4.   The word got out around the farming community that Husker Jones had trained a three-legged pig to do all the chores for him on his farm. Neighbors from far and wide came by to watch the pig round up the cows for milking and chase the horses into the corral at night. Folks were astonished at one of the pig's tricks in which he would suck up a snout-full of water and spray the cows during milking to shoo the flies away. Soon, a reporter heard the story and rushed out to interview farmer Jones.

Jones rocked back in his chair on the front porch of the farm house with a mint julip in his hand and raved about his wonderous pig to the wide-eyed reporter taking notes.

"Why you know, sonny, that pig even saved my grandson's life here a while back," he bragged. "The boy fell in .the swimming pool and almost died. That pig raced over and grabbed him by the shirt and pulled him out. Then, he even jumped up and down on the boy's chest to get his little heart beat'in again. And not a month later, sonny, the barn caught on fire. That smart little pig pushed the fire alarm button and then he got a snout-full of water and even put out the fire before the fire department got here."

"Boy, that's some animal!" exclaimed the reporter. "By the way, how come he's only got three legs?"

Farmer Jones came out of his chair. With a look of amazement at the reporter, he snorted:

Hell fire, city slicker. You think us farmers are stupid? When ya got a pig that smart, ya don't eat him all at once."

5.   Ferdinand the Bull and Ferdinand Jr. were grazing on a grassy hillside one spring day. Ferdinand Jr. looked down at the young cows grazing on the lush pastures below and said:

"Hey, Pop, let's run down the hill, jump that fence, and service one of those hefers down there."

Ferdinand Sr. finished chewing a mouthful of tender grass as he studied his impetuous son. Then he responded:

"Son I got a better idea. Let's say you and I walk down this hill -- and pick up a little grass along the way. Then we can open that gate down there and stroll into the pasture like gentlemen should. And then we can service all them hefers.

6.   When God created man and the animals, he gave them all a normal sex life of 20 years. Man cried out that 20 years was not enough. God told him that it was too late to change the total time assigned to the animal kingdom, but, if he liked, he could talk to the other animals to see if he could trade them out of some of their sex-life time.

Man traded his tree climbing ability to the monkey for 10 years of his sex life. He traded his roar to the lion for 10 years of his time. And he finally convinced the jackass to take most of man's stamina for 10 years of his time.

This explains why man has 20 years of normal sex life, 10 years of monkeying around, 10 years of lion about it, and 10 years of making an ass out of himself.

7.   A giant panda from China came to San Francisco for his vacation. He was strolling around Union Square one evening when one of the City's finest street ladies picked him up and invited him up to her room for the night. The next morning when he was about to leave, she reminded him that he had forgotten something.

The panda from the communist utopia didn't understand what she was suggesting. The lady handed him a pocket dictionary and told him to look up "prostitute." The panda studied this new word for a moment and handed the dictionary back to the lady with the comment: "Look up 'panda' if you please. And thank you for the nice evening." With that, he was out the door.

The empty-handed lady of the night flipped open the dictionary to "panda."   She was sobered by the definition: "Furry animal of the bear family from China. Eats shoots and leaves."

NEWLYWEDS

1. One of the sweetest voices I've ever heard on radio called me one night to tell me about her wedding night. She had been listening to callers on my show moan about the difficulties that young couples were having who couldn't afford the high price of homes and had to live in apartments. She began by telling us that she and her new husband were so poor that they had to move in with her mother on their wedding night.

The mother, of course, offered her upstairs bedroom to the newlyweds. She was sleeping on the couch downstairs. Suddenly, she heard a scream from above, then a thud on the floor, and then loud sobbing from the upstairs bedroom. She jumped up and raced for the stairway, only to be met by her new son-in-law running down the stairs in his untied bathrobe.

"Mother-in-law, mother-in-law," he said frantically, tears glistening in his eyes. "Mary screamed and fainted, and now she is sitting up in bed covering her eyes and crying -- and I don't know why. All I did was take off my clothes to go to bed."

The mother-in-law thought for a moment about her wedding night long ago. Her poor, innocent, virgin daughter was clearly experiencing the same shock of seeing a naked man for the first time. She smiled to herself at how quickly she got over that minor trauma.

"Now Johnny, don't you worry about it. Mary will get over the surprise of seeing you for the first time," she said. "Now you dry your tears on your bathrobe and go up and comfort her and everything will be alright in a day or two."

Johnny nodded his appreciation for her wisdom. He picked up the hem of his bathrobe to dry his tears. It fell open at the waist. His mother-in-law screamed and fainted.

2.   It was the wedding night for Princess Diana and Prince Charles. Women callers on my talk show were bubbling with enthusiasm over the romance of the royal wedding and what a storybook scene it was that handsome Prince Charles had chosen a beautiful commoner for his bride. Then came an old salt with this story he said his dad had told him about humble women:

The King decided to marry a commoner chosen from all the beautiful maidens of the land. On their wedding night, they were bedded down in the King's elegant chambers. In the darkness, from under the covers, the overjoyed bride gasped: "My Lord, my Lord, d-d-do th-th-the poor people do this?"

"Why yes, my dear," whispered the gentle King to his bride.

"Wa-wa-well, it must be stopped," she commanded.   "It's much too good for them."

3.   For reasons I can never figure out, the subject on my show one night turned to "How did you tell people about your first baby." Most callers admitted to pestering people with pictures of their first born -- and then couldn't remember what they had said or done about their next kids that came along. One bachelor held back with this story until the end of the hour:

He said that the couple next door had been trying to have a baby for ten years. Then, finally, the couple succeeded. Nine months later he was walking out to his car one morning when the new father came running over and thrust a big cigar in his hand. "George, you've got to see this baby boy of mine," he gushed. "The kid's got the biggest arms you've ever seen. And legs! This kid's got legs like a linebacker. And balls! ---- why the kid bawls all night long."

4. And then came the cruel one from a midnight caller:

Henry, a quiet bookkeeper at the office, and a very nice, sweet guy, finally had his first child after fifteen years of marriage. The normally shy and quiet bookkeeper was bubbling with pride to all his office friends.

Henry offered a cigar to the office jokster, the outside salesman known as T.J.. This wise guy smarted off with: "Well, well, Henry, your wife had a baby, you say? I wonder who the father is (chuckle, chuckle)."

Quiet little Henry reflected for a moment on this vulgar suggestion. Then, with a condescending smile at the cruel idiot, Henry calmly responded: "T.J., my guess would be that it's your wife."

"What do you mean by that?" T.J. laughed, as he fell into the trap.

"Oh, it just sounds resonable from what I hear around the office," Henry answered with a tone of remorse. "They tell me she has been screwing everybody in town while you're travelling."

5. A listener called to inform me that one of the most common complaints heard in the bedroom actually came from the very first newlyweds, Adam and Eve.

According to her, Adam was awakened from a sound sleep one afternoon in the Garden of Eden by the voice of God booming down from the heavens.

"Adam. I've decided to give you a companion. I've taken one of your ribs to make this companion for you," said the voice of God.

"What is this companion called?" asked Adam as he rubbed the sleep out of his eyes.

"It's a she, and she is called woman," answered God.

"Well, where is this thing called woman?" asked Adam.

"Over behind the bushes.   She's waiting to meet you," answered God.

Adam got up and hurried over behind the bushes to meet his new companion.   Shortly, he came back to his resting place and looked up to the heavens.

"God. Are you there?" he pleaded with a puzzled look on his face.

"Yes, Adam. What is it you want now?"

"God. What's a headache?"

CONDOMS

1. Young Joe Sixpack rolls up to a country drugstore in his pickup with his girlfriend cuddling next to him. She squeezes his arm affectionately as he slides out the door. He rushes into the store and asks the clerk: "How much for a condom?"

She smiles knowingly and answers: "Seventy-five cents plus tax."

Joe digs into his Levis and hauls out his change. He glances anxiously back at his girlfriend waiting in the pickup. "Skip the tax," he says. "I'll wire it on."

2. Farmer John Goodseed is worried about the latest weather report that is predicting heavy frost for the morning. The frost will surely damage his ripening crop of prized seed corn. Then he is struck with an ingenious idea. He races to the country drugstore and orders a gross of condoms from his old-time friend, Henry the druggist. The smiling druggist carefully counts out the 144 rubbers as he grins at his fellow church-goer, Goodseed.

Back at the farm, the clever Goodseed carefully stretches one condom over each ear of his seed corn ripening in the field. Goodseed's corn is the only crop in the valley that suffers no damage when the frost hits the next morning.

A week later, heavy frost is again predicted. Goodseed returns to the drugstore and orders another gross of rubbers. As the druggist is counting out the next batch, Goodseed casually comments: "By the way, Henry, you were one short in that last batch. I counted."

The druggist interrupted his counting, winked at his friend, and said: "Well darn, Henry, I'm really sorry if I spoiled your weekend."

3.   A small Texas condom manufacturing company received a surprising order for one million condoms from the Soviet Union. Even more surprising were the specifications. The size ordered was three inches in diameter by twelve inches long -- minimum. Not to be outdone by these arrogant Russians, the proud Texan stationed a worker at the end of the assembly line to stamp each condom "MEDIUM" before they were packaged.

4.   A handsome young sailor on leave in San Francisco met a local sorority girl. After a romantic day of sightseeing and dinner at the Cliff House, they ended up petting furiously in the front seat of her sports car as they parked at Ocean Beach. Suddenly, she whispered in his ear: "How come you sailors have two rows of buttons on your pants?"

He whispered back, "Don't you know? All sailors have two of them."

"Ah, come on, you're kidding me," she answers.

"Well, I'll show you," he says, whereupon he proceeds to unbutton the left side of his skivies. He pulls it out to show her.

She exclaims: "Oh my, isn't that something." The smile on her face tells him that it's time for action. She watches intently as he confidently applies a condom.

Later, as he buttons up his pants, she asks in all seriousness: "But where is the other one?"

"Oh, you want to see the other one?" He unbuttons the right side of his skivies and pulls it out that side.

"I'll be darned," she giggles. "But why is that one so much smaller than the first one?"

With the authority of the Captain on the bridge, the sailor shrugs and responds: "Ah, this one always pouts when I show the other one first."

5. And what do the little kids learn in school these days? A grammar school kid heard one of the above condom jokes. He soon called the show with these questions:

"Dr. Wattenburg, how come big pencils don't make little pencils?"

"Darned if I know."

"It's easy. Big pencils have a rubber on the end."

"And how come big trains don't make little trains?"

"OK. Shock me."

"Don't you know that trains always pull out on time?"

A BAD DAY

1.   A sailor on leave in San Francisco called in to offer this hard luck story to humble a number of previous callers who had been grousing about the minor woes in their lives:

A sailor walked into a beachfront bar in San Francisco on a cold, foggy afternoon. He was wearing a heavy navy peacoat. He sat down at the bar and rested his head in his hands with a look of complete dejection.   When the bartender approached, the sailor growled: "Give me a triple whiskey -- and bring the bottle."   The bartender returned with the bottle and said politely, "You must have had a bad day, I guess. What's the problem, son?"

The sailor took a big gulp of whiskey and answered, "I'll show you."   He reached under the left side of his peacoat and pulled out a miniature grand piano. From the right side, he pulled out a little one-foot tall piano player, dressed in tux and top hat. He tipped over an empty glass on the bar as a stool for the tiny piano player. When he tapped the glass, the piano player pounded out a piano concerto.

The bartender was flabbergasted.   "Good Lord," he exclaimed, "That's unbelievable. "I'd be the happiest guy in the world if I were you."

The sad sailor said, "That's what you think. I was down at Ocean Beach this morning, before the fog came in, and a bottle washed up on the beach. I pulled the cork out of the bottle and a genie popped out. He told me I could have the one wish I have wanted all my life because I had set him free. But only one wish."

He paused to empty the whiskey bottle and then looked down at the busy little piano player. In his drunken stupor he murmured: "Wouldn't you know it, I of all people get a hard-of-hearing genie -- and I end up with this damn twelve-inch pianist."

2.   A few calls later on the same show, another voice of wisdom topped the show with:

"I want to tell those poor guys with their hard luck stories what my dad told me when I left home for my first job. He said, "Son, always remember that you ain't got real trouble in this life until your wife, your girlfriend, and the note at the bank are all overdue."

3.   The above reminded me of a gem of wisdom from my dad when he was sixty-five. We were in the Greenville Coffee Shop for breakfast at five-thirty in the morning, as usual, before we began another workday in the logging woods of Northern California. A frisky waitress who had known him for years teased him as she brought the coffee: "How's your sex life these days, Bill?"

My tired old dad looked up at her and said: "Sweety, when a man gets my age he ought'a lose his testicles instead of his teeth. He can still use his teeth."

4. The club tennis pro was dressing in the locker room one day when he noticed one of the better-known members, a rich businessman, struggling to wiggle into a ladies girdle. Poor guy. He's got a bad back, the pro thought to himself. He shook his head sympathetically toward the disabled senior member and commented:

"Hey, I know what a bad back feels like. I had the same problem myself a few years ago and had to wear a brace for months. How long you been wearing that girdle?"

The man struggling to get into the girdle gave him a sorrowful look and mumbled: "Ever since my wife found it under the front seat of my car."

5.   My father told me this one when I was sixteen. He had been listening to me cry over the loss of my first girlfriend:

A young tom cat had grown fond of taking afternoon naps near the railroad tracks to rest up for his next night of chasing females.   He had discovered that the iron rails retained the warmth from the mid-day sun long after the cool breezes of winter chilled the air about him. He had become so comfortable with the passing trains that he seldom moved as the train wheels rolled by overhead within inches of his body.

One day, as he snuggled close to an iron rail, his tail twitched in his sleep and it came to rest over the rail. Shortly, the train came along and cut off his tail. The tom cat awoke in a fury. Without thinking, he stuck his head over the rail to retrieve his tail and the next wheel cut off his head. End of story.

I looked at my dad with no small amount of disgust. How could he think that his dumb story about a cat could possibly soothe the hurt that I was feeling over the greatest loss of my young life? "So what the hell does that mean?" I asked.

"Well boy, you gotta learn not to learn lose your head over a little piece of tail."

OFF COLOR SHOCKERS

Sometimes a caller on talk radio will slip in a clever off-color joke on the air and the slow-witted host doesn't catch on to the punch line until it's too late to hit the censor button. The host can be in real trouble if the joke happens to offend some ethnic group. Here are a couple that taught me to stay on my toes.

1. This one got by me one night during a serious discussion of "training dangerous animals". Was I relieved to discover later that my listeners in San Francisco had a sense of humor.

The caller identified himself as an attendant at the San Diego Zoo who was on vacation in San Francisco to attend the Gay Freedom Day festivities. He offered this story to prove that some dangerous animals could be tamed:

A burly alligator trainer from Florida walked into a San Francisco all-male bar with his small pet alligator. The bartender immediately exclaimed: "Get that thing the hell out of here."

The guy protested: "Don't worry, he's harmless. I'll show you." He pried open the alligator's jaws and put his head in the alligator's mouth. "See," he said. "He won't bite."

The bartender was still unimpressed, and one of the customers chuckled, "Ya, but I'll bet you wouldn't put your penis in his jaws like that."

The guy unbuttoned his pants and proceeded to place his prize between the alligator's jaws. Then, to display his extreme confidence in his alligator, he pounded the alligator of the top of the head with his fist a couple of times. The alligator's jaws never closed.

The proud alligator trainer turned to the doubting crowd and said: "Anyone else want to try it?"   A fellow at the back of the room raised his hand and said: "I will -- if you promise not to hit me on the head so hard."

2.   And another one:

"Bill Wattenburg. Do you know what they call a guy who doesn't leave a tip for a Chinese waiter?"

"No."

"A PLICK!"

PUT DOWNS FOR POMPOUS MALES

1. One night I was solving popular riddles and math puzzles on talk radio. Admittedly, I had been a little arrogant with a few callers who gave me obviously trivial problems that I had heard a hundred times before. Then came a sweet female voice which asked:

"Bill, have you ever read the serial number on a condom?"

Somewhat exasperated, I snapped: "Lady, they don't put serial numbers on condoms."

Just as I suddenly remembered this voice from the past -- too late -- she let me have it: "Well, Bill dear, that's because as I remember you never had to roll one up far enough to see it!"

2. Two business women were walking down the street one day when they spotted a large bullfrog on the sidewalk. "Help me! Ladies, please help me!" cried the frog. "I was once a handsome young stockbroker. I was very popular with the ladies. Some said I was a real stud. But then a mean witch put a curse on me and turned me into a frog. All you have to do is give me a kiss and I'll be transformed back into a man. You won't be sorry ladies, I guarantee you that."

One of the women reached down and picked him up. She quickly stuffed the frog into her handbag. The other one asked: "But aren't you going to kiss him?"

The first woman shook her head firmly and answered: "Hell no! Who needs another stud around? He's worth a fortune as a talking frog."

3.   A spry grandmother from Oregon called the talk show to tell about a smart woman's favorite animals. "A smart lady has a mink in the closet, a jaguar in the garage, a tiger in the bedroom, and a jackass like you Bill Wattenburg to pay for it all."

4.   I began as a talk show host on KGO radio, San Francisco, in 1971 after writing a silly satire on the sexual follies of my generation which became a surprising best-seller. As author Will Harvey, I had appeared on over 145 radio and TV interview shows around the country. Naturally, when I returned to the Bay Area there were a lot of women who wanted to tease me (or curse me) about the outrageous exploits of Will Harvey in the book. On my third appearance as a host on KGO radio, a young lady called to tell me that she was a flight attendant and that she had met me on a flight. She said she didn't know how to respond to me at the time, but after thinking it over she now had a story to tell me. I knew instantly that I was in trouble, but it was too late. I couldn't cut her off the air without angering the audience. Here was her story for me.

"Bill, my old uncle was a prospector in the Mojave desert years ago, and he used to ride around on his donkey looking for gold in the mountains. Well, as you know, a donkey in biblical times was called an ass. So, he rode around on his trusty ass year after year.

One day he had climbed high up on a cliff to inspect some rocks. He lost his footing and fell down the cliff and broke both of his arms. He would have perished out there, except that he was able to climb on his trusty little ass which took him into the Mojave hospital.

But wouldn't you know it, they wouldn't treat him because he had no money. However, that didn't stop my crusty old uncle. He picked up a pencil in his mouth off the nurse's table and wrote a check on a blank piece of paper with his mouth. Then he gave it to his trusty ass to take to the bank.

But wouldn't you know it, the bank wouldn't cash the check because it wasn't a personalized check." End of story.

"Well, what's the message of your story?" I asked.

She calmly responded: "Bill Wattenburg, alias Will Harvey, you of all people should know the moral of this story. Don't you ever again write a check with your mouth that your ass can't cash."

5. The above story brought a quick call from a young lady who said she had met one of our more flamboyant TV hosts in town, or rather, he had introduced himself to her as follows:

She was waiting for a bus at a street corner near the TV station one afternoon. He pulled up in front of the station in his sports car and hopped out. As he was walking toward the station entrance, he spotted her and turned in her direction. She knew he probably expected to be recognized. Soon, he was standing beside her.

She deliberately took no notice of him. She knew he would try some opening gambit to start a conversation. And he did.

A large German shepherd, tied to a lamp post across the street, was washing his hind leg with his tongue while its owner was inside a store. The enterprising TV host was being very cool and watching the dog while he pretended not to notice her beside him.

"See that dog over there? Sure wish I could do that, ha, ha," he chuckled to get her attention.

By the time they glanced back at the dog, the dog had changed the target of his washing operation. She said that she just couldn't resist the comment: "Well, I guess, if you're into that sort of thing, mister. But I'd pet him first, if I were you."

6.   Suzy from the typing pool, straight out of high school, was burning up the keyboard during her noon hour trying to finish a marketing report. The department secretary had quit in a huff that morning after the latest confrontation with Mr. Slick, the marketing manager, who had the habit of leering at women in the office. Suzy was wearing a miniskirt and a low-cut blouse very becoming of her youthful figure. She had been warned about Slick. She hunched over close to her typewriter and kept very busy each time he passed by her desk.

Eventually, the sly Mr. Slick was leaning over her desk and leering down her blouse. Suzy paid no attention to him. Slick struggled to think of something to say to draw her attention.

First, he commented on how little cloth it took to cover a lady's body with the modern fashions. "Personally, I think a great body like yours looks best with nothing on -- under the right circumstances, ha, ha."   Suzy looked up to give him a supercilious smile as her fingers raced over the keys.

This was a come-on for old Slick. Now he had to find a way to engage her in conversation. He'd get her talking, one way or the other.

"You know, I always feel sorry for girls for all the junk they have to wear -- you know, brassieres and the like. It's a crime. A guy can take his shirt off on a hot day like this and enjoy the weather." Still no comment from Suzy. She popped her bubble gum as she hit the carriage return on the fly.

Slick's next inane opening was: "Say, what do you think is the most worthless thing a pretty young girl like you would have to wear these days?"

Suzy had heard enough. She finished the last sentence on the page, rested her tired hands in her lap, and gave Slick a sweet smile. "Oh, I'd say a married man about your age."

These next two came from women flight attendants who were not impressed with an airline pilot who called my show to complain about the problems of deregulation of the airlines. At one point, however, he chuckled that there were still a few advantages to being a pilot -- such as the lovely flight attendants on lay-overs.

7.   A flight attendant called to tell us about a pilot who would sometimes leave the cockpit to come back and pester her with offers of romance when they got to their lay-over. She tried to ignore his advances while she raced in and out of the galley with meals for the passengers, but he would continue to try to make small talk with her as she worked.

He was standing in her way in the aisle as she tried to go by with an armful of trays. He came up with one of his usual inane comments designed to get her talking:

"Gee, you look good wearing glasses. Can you see without them?"

In a voice loud enough for all the nearby passengers to hear, she answered: "Without these glasses, sweety, I can't see a man until he is on top of me."

8.   An airline passenger called me to tell about an episode that he observed that convinced him that he shouldn't pester flight attendants. He was seated in the first class section near the galley on a flight from New York to L.A.. A middle-aged playboy with a hairy chest and gold chains hanging around his neck was trying to impress a cute flight attendant that he could put her in the movies. He claimed that he was a movie producer on his way to film his next big hit.

He was standing with his arm over the door of the galley as she ducked under him with a load of trays in her hands. Each time she passed by he insisted that she should visit him at his Beverly Hills pad on her lay-over in L.A.. On her third trip out of the galley, she stopped, smiled sweetly, poked him in the chest with her finger, and said for all to hear:

"You know something, Pop. You're all flap and no throttle. You had better sit down before you spin out."

9. Two proper single ladies, Suzy and Mary, were having a drink after work in a country western bar one evening. Several real cowboys came over to ask them to dance. The ladies politely refused because they were tired. Then Suzy's former boyfriend wandered over in his new Macy's cowboy outfit with an emormous silver belt buckle. He had made a bet with the other guys that he could get her on her feet.

"Hey, Suzy dear, you still got a little action left in you, haven't you?" he announced in a loud voice for his buddies to hear.

Suzy shook her head at him in disgust and snapped back:

"As I recall, you'd probably fall asleep on your feet."

Her old boyfriend spun around in anger and stomped away.

Her girlfriend, Mary, asked: "Why is he wearing that big belt buckle?"

Suzy couldn't resist the urge to drive the last nail in his coffin as she answered loud enough for all his buddies at the bar to hear. "That big, silver-plated belt buckle is just a tombstone for his dead pecker."

10. A sweet lady called my talk show with this stinging observation after a series of callers had been discussing the subject of male sexual aggressiveness.

"Bill, do you know why most men like you give their penis a name?" she asked.

"Why no," I answered with some bewilderment. "The thought never entered my mind."

"Because, Bill dear, I'm sure you don't want to go through life having ninety-five percent of your decisions made by a total stranger."

11. A go-go executive came home early for the first time in months. He announced to his wife: "Honey, I want to make love to you in the worst way."

As she was untying her apron and moving toward the bedroom, she answered, "You do."

BATTERED WOMEN

1. Sadie Anderson was the assistant station master for the Rocky Mountain Railroad at Whistle Stop, Colorado, which meant that for ten years she had done all the work while the alcoholic station master slept it off in the back room. Then he died one day. He was a bachelor with no family, no friends in Whistle Stop. Sadie just put him in a Cardboard box and shipped him to his relatives in Denver. No one knew the difference, except for a few railroad hands. She never told the railroad bosses.

Then, a nosey reporter broke the story. By that time, Sadie had been doing the station master's job for three years, all by herself. The railroad bosses were going to fire her immediately -- until they discovered that they had sent two commendations to the Whistle Stop station master for excellent performance in the past two years. Their public relations department came to the rescue. Here was the chance of a lifetime to publicize the company's equal opportunity program. A special ceremony was scheduled at Whistle Stop whereby the company president, Mr. Royal Cocksman, would give Sadie an award for her performance.

Mr. Cocksman arrived in Whistle Stop on the appointed day and immediately requested a private audience with Sadie. After a few amenities, he noticed that Sadie had a rather nice figure for her age. "Say, where can a man find a little fun in this town?" he asked slyly.

"What kind of fun you have in mind, Mr. Cocksman?" She asked very formally.

Cocksman winked at Sadie and answered: "Oh, you know. A lady who enjoys the finer things in life with a gentleman who has some money in his pocket."

Sadie thought for a moment and suddenly had a bright idea. "Oh! Do I know just the right lady for you, Mr. Cocksman," she exclaimed. "Down the tracks a ways there is an old abandoned railroad tunnel. In that tunnel lives a strange lady, but the fellows say that she is young and absolutely gorgeous. Well, about five o'clock each evening, she commences to give out a mating call for a lover. She goes WOOO, WOOO, WOOOO, at least three times. They say that if you take your clothes off and run into the tunnel, she will treat you to sexual pleasures out of this world."

Mr. Cocksman was beaming with anticipation. He patted Sadie on the back and told her how much he liked a station master who knew how to take care of upper management when they came into town. She would do well in the company.

The next morning, the Rocky Mountain newspapers bannered the headline: NAKED RAILROAD EXECUTIVE RUN DOWN BY FREIGHT TRAIN IN TUNNEL.

2. A husband came home from work one evening to be greeted by the smell of dirty diapers stacked on the floor in the laundry room. "Dear, would you help me fix the washing machine?" asked his distraught wife. "It broke down this morning and I can't get anyone to come out until next week."

"Who in the hell do you think I am, the Maytag Man?" growled her husband. "Where's my dinner?"

The next evening, he came home to find his wife and kids gone. An hour later they dragged in. "I'm so sorry, Dear," she apologized. "The car broke down in the supermarket parking lot and we had to walk home. Would you fix it for me after dinner?"

"Who in the hell do you think I am? Mr. Goodwrench?" he snapped. She said no more and prepared his dinner.

On the third night, he came home to find the car in the driveway and the washing machine running in the laundry room. "How did you get those fixed?" he asked as she poured his martini.

The happy wife responded: "Oh, the nice bachelor who lives next door fixed them for me."

"What did he charge us?" demanded the husband.

"Oh, he said I could cook him a good steak dinner sometime -- or, I could take him to bed. He's such a funny guy."

"You didn't give him that T-bone that I've been saving in the refrigerator, did you?" demanded her husband.

"Dear, who in the hell do you think I am? Betty Crocker?

3.   A housewife complained to her husband that she had no money to buy even little things for herself after he wasted his paycheck on drinking and gambling. He growled that she could get a job if she wasn't satisfied. She pointed out that she had no training for a job because she had spent twenty years taking care of him and raising the kids. His answer was that she could go out on the street like the rest of the working girls, ha, ha.

One night, she put on her best clothes and did just that. She came in at three in the morning with a big smile on her face. Her husband woke up in a drunken stupor and snidely asked: "How much did you make?"

"Twenty dollars and ten cents," she answered proudly.

"Ten cents! Who was the cheap bastard that gave you ten cents? he chuckled.

"Oh, all of them," she smiled.

4.   A grandmother who heard the "ten cents" story above called to tell me how she had shaped up her cheap-skate husband early in their marriage. They were strolling down Fifth Avenue in New York one evening when she spotted a modestly-priced fur coat in the window of a department store. She pleaded with him to buy it for her because she had nothing warm to wear in the cold New York winters.   He complained that it was a waste of money because she could wear one of his jackets if she had to go out of their apartment.

She turned to him and opened her blouse to reveal her cleavage. He was stunned by her strange behavior on a public street.

"See this," she said as she pointed to her chest. "Before I married you, this was my hope chest. After I married you, it became your tool chest. And if I don't get that coat, it's going to be a community chest."

5.   Mabel always had a difficult time buying presents for her airline captain husband.   He had seen and done almost everything in the world. His birthday was coming up. She vowed to try extra hard to find something for him that he had never seen before.

She had the bright idea to look at pets. He had never had a pet before, as far as she knew. She walked into a pet store that specialized in exotic pets and began looking around at the snakes, lizards, and monkeys from around the world. Suddenly, she heard a tremendous growl from the back room. She raced over to ask the owner what it was. He told her that it was a Wollybugger.

"A Wollybugger!   I never heard of such a thing," she exclaimed. "Can I see it?"

The owner pulled back the curtain to reveal a gorilla-like animal with long fangs for teeth and sharp claws. It was securely chained to the concrete wall.

"Don't get close to it," warned the owner. "It's normally very calm and loving. However, if you tell it the name of anything, it will attack.

"When does it do that?" she asked excitedly.

"I'll show you," said the owner. He grabbed a rabbit and shouted: "Wollybugger, rabbit!"

The Wollybugger snatched the rabbit and ripped it to shreds with its claws.

"Oh my God," she screeched. "I have to have it. Show me once again how you do that."

The owner held up a small pig. "Wollybugger, pig!" he said. The Wollybugger ripped the pig to shreds.

She jumped up and down with joy. Surely, her difficult husband had never seen anything like this. She paid the owner the thousand dollars he asked and took the Wollybugger home.

That night her husband came home late. As he walked into the darkened bedroom, he saw what looked like a hairy man in bed with his wife in the dim light.

"Who the hell is that in bed with you?" he roared.

She answered: "Be calm dear. It's a special surprise for you. It's called a Wollybugger.

Her husband growled: "Wollybugger, my ass!"

6. A disgruntled male caller to my talk show carried on at great length about how he had noticed that women nowadays seemed to be meaner and much more grouchy than in the "old days" when he was young. He blamed it on the feminist movement. I knew that this would stimulate a proper response before long. Sure enough, soon came a call from a lady who said:

"Bill, the men in our society won't allow a woman to belch, snore, or fart. Naturally, she has to bitch once in a while-- otherwise, she'd blow up.

7. And the above was quickly followed by:

"Do you know why young women don't fart?" asked a giggling lady.

"No."

"Because we don't get an asshole until we get married."

NASTY WOMEN

1. A man called my show to tell us about a friend of his who had slaved for thirty years to support an unappreciative wife who had spent every penny he had ever made on trinkets for herself. He loved her dearly, but he was reaching the end of his rope when he discovered that she had spent the last of their savings on a fickle, pure-bred cat that she had to take to the vet every week.

But then the cat suddenly died. His anger turned to sorrow for his wife, as usual. Her birthday was coming up, and he decided to buy her another cat. The next night he brought home a sweet, gentle cat that he was sure would please her. She threw a fit and screamed:

"Get that horrible looking thing out of here. And you can sleep in the garage along with it."

The next night, he brought her some flowers for her birthday to buy his way in the door. She promptly threw them in the waste basket with the comment:

"You must have picked those along the highway on your way home." He was heartbroken as she demanded that he sleep in the garage again.

The third night, he presented her with a shoe box wrapped with a black ribbon. She opened it to find six furry little kittens inside. "What the hell are these for?" she demanded.

Her tired husband turned as he walked toward the garage and responded: "My dear, those are the pallbearers for your dead pussy."

2.   One night on KGO Radio, I was taking calls from women who were rightfully not happy with the way they were treated by the men in their lives at times. For the most part, they considered their relationships to be generally satisfying, but they wanted some improvements. Then a woman called who identified herself as hating all men. She began by saying that she normally wouldn't stoop to even talk to a man, let alone have a relationship with one. Then, with a long string of expletives, she ripped into all women who had anything to do with men. I let her scream her vindictiveness without comment from me because she was her own worst enemy in front of this audience.

The next caller was a woman who identified herself as a working housewife. She commented: "You know Bill, that last caller's problem began when she was born."

I asked: "How's that?"

"With a knowing chuckle, she said: "When the doctor slapped her on the butt to get her lungs going, he knocked her balls off!"

3.   Another caller told me about a high-society lady who pulled up to a country restaurant in her new Cadillac. She walked into the bar with her pet rabbit on a leash. She sat down at a table and commanded the lone bartender to come over and serve her immediately, even though he was obviously busy tending to the oldtimers seated at the bar.

He sat down the drinks he was about to serve to others and approached her table. "Well, what will it be for the pig?" he asked.

Indignantly she retorted, "Can't you see that he is a rabbit, you damn fool?"

"Lady, I was talking to the rabbit."

4.   Neat and tidy George married Alice because she had convinced him that she was a terrific housekeeper and great social companion.   However,   within a few months after their marriage, Alice began to neglect everything except her soap operas and candy which she gobbled all day.   Soon, she was sixty pounds overweight.   She wore the same clothes a week at a time, and let the dishes stack up until the ants were swarming into the house.

Poor George hired a housekeeper to clean up the house and told his wife she would have to see a counselor about her emotional problems.

The counselor took one look at her and decided that she had a self-esteem problem.   She had to improve her appearance before he would have any chance to deal with her emotional problems.   Husband George dutifully shelled out a thousand dollars so she could have her hair done, buy new clothes, and enter a weight control program the counselor recommended. Alice had her hair done, but spent the rest of the money on a year's supply of chocolates that she hid away in the basement.

A week later, the frustrated counselor again told her that she had to present herself to her husband with a more feminine appearance if she expected him to take any interest in her.   "Go home and take a bath, fix your hair, and buy a sexy nightgown -- you know, something with a plunging neckline so you can meet him at the door in something exciting."

Alice reluctantly followed his instructions; but, instead of buying a new nightgown, she found an old one she had discarded on the bedroom floor.   It had a plunging back.   What the hell, she thought.   I'll just put it on backwards. He'll never know the difference.

George walked in that night and immediately noticed the usual candy wrappers scattered on the living room floor.   He sat down in front of the television and turned on the news.   His wife quickly brushed her hair and made her entrance out of the bedroom. She stood in front of him with her substantial clevage bulging out of her turned-around nightgown and asked: "George, don't you notice anything different?"

"Yah, you combed your hair for a change." he said as he looked her over. "And you have your nightgown on backwards."

"How do you know that, dear?" she asked with surprise in her voice.

Her husband shook his head slowly in final disgust and answered: "Because the brown stains are on the front."

CORPORATE WORLD

1.   Charlie Climber had just been appointed president and chief operating officer of his company, the culmination of twenty years of hard work and single-minded dedication to the firm that had first hired him as a stock clerk. Today, he would be attending his first board meeting as the new president. He had labored day and night to prepare a business plan for how he would reorganize the company management to double its profits.

Unfortunately, after a limp introduction by the board chairman and owner of the company, poor Charlie never got a word in edgewise during the rest of the board meeting. The chairman did all the talking. Charlie was crushed.

After the meeting, Charlie asked a friend on the board why he had been ignored by the chairman.   The wise old board member thought a moment, put an arm around Charlie's shoulder and said: "Charlie, I want to tell you a little story you should never forget.

There was once an old gorilla at the zoo who was getting pretty tired, so the zoo brought in a young gorilla to please the crowds. The young gorilla arrived and immediately put on a great show for the folks before he even unpacked his bags. The old gorilla sat in his cage and never moved.

That evening the zookeeper brought the food.   The old gorilla got a washtub full of succulent fruit. But the young gorilla got only a small plate with one banana, one apple, and a few grapes. The young gorilla decided that they hadn't been expecting him so soon, and he let it pass.

The young gorilla put on a tremendous show again the next day. When the food came that night, he still got only a quarter of what they fed the old gorilla. The young gorilla was furious. He rattled his cage until the zookeeper came over and asked what the problem was.

The young gorilla explained how he was being unrewarded for all his efforts while the old gorilla sat on his ass in the sun and got washtubs full of succulent fruit for doing nothing. The zookeeper shook his head at the naive young gorilla and responded:

"You got to understand something, fellow. This is a zoo. And this here zoo is like a corporation. In a corporation, there is room for just one gorilla. Son, they got you on the books as a chimpanzee."

2.   Jerry, a recent graduate from the Stanford Business School, attended his first corporate cocktail party hosted by the president of the company that had just hired him. The gathering at the president's house was delightful, and Jerry decided it was time to join the ranks of top management and become a drinking man. He tried his first martini -- and his second -- and his third.

He woke up in his apartment the next morning with a horrible headache. Then he recalled a strange dream in which he had entered a bathroom at the president's house the night before and discovered that all the fixtures -- and especially the toilet -- were gold plated! His curiosity obsessed him until he decided that he had to find out for sure.

He called the president's house. The president's wife answered the phone. Humbly, he inquired: "Mrs. Jones, I hate to bother you like this, but there is something that impressed me a great deal at your beautiful home last night. Do you have a gold plated toilet in your downstairs bathroom?"

There was a long moment of silence on the other end of the phone. Then management trainee Jerry heard a deep sigh from the president's wife before she hollered over her shoulder to someone in the house: "George, the guy who shit in your tuba is on the phone."

3.   Archibald Gladhand, the new gung-ho executive VP from Arizona, was having a great time hustling the young secretaries at the XYZ Corporation Christmas party in Minneapolis. This was his first opportunity to meet the working level girls socially since he had joined the company. He was on his fifth glass of high-octane punch and patting tender bottoms as quick as he could corral them. Then three of the young ladies cornered him and informed him that they were going to go ice fishing. It was an old mid-winter tradition in Minnesota, and great fun, they assured him. They had already packed fishing poles and warm coats in their car for the occasion.

Gladhand quickly agreed to go along. The ladies put him in their car and drove him to the site. They woke him from his drunken stupor, gave him an ice saw and fishing pole, and told him to cut a hole for them. They were going to scout some other areas and would be back shortly.

Gladhand was sawing on the ice when he heard a booming voice from high above: "THERE ARE NO FISH UNDER THE ICE." He looked around and above, but saw no one, and decided that he was just hearing things. So he went back to sawing on the ice.

Again, the booming voice said: "THERE ARE NO FISH UNDER THE ICE."

This time, he was shaken. He knew he was not imagining things. "Is that you, God?" he asked.

The booming voice came back: "NO, YOU DAMN FOOL, THIS IS THE MANAGER OF THE ICE SKATING RINK."

4.   Henry Jones had worked on the assembly line at the XYZ Pickle factory for three years. He loved his work. His job was to grab the gorgeous pickles off the assembly line and feed them to the pickle slicer. Some thought him to be a little strange because

no one else could stand this repetitive job for more than a few days. Little did they know that Henry was obsessed with the idea of sticking his penis into the pickle slicer.

One day, he couldn't help himself. He did it -- right in front of everybody. Naturally, the assembly line came to a halt as the supervisors rushed to the gory scene. They quickly rescued Henry from the pickle slicer and carried him out of the building as his fellow workers stood around in shocked disbelief.

A manager who soon arrived was worried about down time in the plant. He immediately asked: "What happened to the pickle slicer?"

A nearby worker shrugged his shoulders and answered: "Ah, they fired her too."

5.   A curious tourist from Ohio visiting San Francisco climbed to the top deck of the Bank of America building one windy day to see what the view was like. There he encountered two well-dressed young businessmen eating their bag lunches and sharing a bottle of wine. He approached them with a question: "Pardon me for interrupting, but does the wind always blow this hard in San Francisco?"

The taller of the two businessmen sat down his wine glass, thought for a moment, and answered: "As a matter of fact, Mister, the wind blows so hard between the skyscrapers here that you can jump over the side of this building and it will stop you from falling before you reach the tenth floor."

The tourist was incredulous. "Ah, come on. I don't believe that for a minute."

The businessman stepped over to the edge of the railing and said: "Watch me." He jumped over the side as the startled tourist raced to see him go down.

Sure enough, he stopped in mid-air at the tenth floor, reached over to a window and crawled back into the building.

When the businessman appeared back at the top deck, the excited tourist immediately asked: "Do you think I could do that? The folks back home would never believe it."

"Sure, no problem. Here, give me your camera. I'll take a picture of you as you go down."

The tourist took a deep breath, closed his eyes and jumped over the railing. He fell straight to the sidewalk and was splattered on the concrete. The young businessman who had given the ill-fated demonstration calmly raised his wine glass to continue his lunch where he had left off. His partner scowled at him and said: "Superman, two glasses of wine and you turn into a real asshole."

THE COLLEGE SCENE

1.   The talk show callers were focusing on the merits of the better known universities in the U.S. one night. A fortunate high school senior who had been accepted at both Cal and Stanford called in to give us the benefit of his belief that the private universites were far superior to the state universites because the private school graduates made a lot more money. I was thinking to myself about the thousands of other desperate students listening who would be happy to be able to attend any university, public or private. Then came a young woman who said she was a student at Cal Berkeley. She had a story for the naive high school senior:

Saint Peter materialized on earth to examine the morals of our new generation. He selected a student at Harvard, a student at Stanford, and a student at Cal. He told them that he would grant them any degree of success they wanted if they would tell him their true desires.

The Harvard student said he wanted to be a Congressman and then run for President. The Stanford student said he wanted to be a rich stockbroker with a mansion in Hillsborough that had a six car garage full of sports cars and gorgeous ladies in every bedroom.

Finally, Saint Peter turned to the Cal student, a young woman majoring in biochemistry. She plucked a loose thread from her tattered Levis and absentmindedly checked the soles of her worn-out tennis shoes while she thought it over for a moment. Then she answered: "Tell you what, Pete. Just give me about twenty dollars worth of costume jewelry -- and that Stanford boy's telephone number."

2.   A senior in the fraternity often bragged that he was an escape artist on a par with the great Houdini. The fraternity had planned a beer party at a ranch nearby where they could drink until they dropped without the cops bothering them. There, he promised to put on a show for the sorority girls they had invited.

Two hours into the party, the beer was sloshing in their bellies and they were throwing their beer cans at the cows for fun. The escape artist announced that he wanted them to tie him up behind the barn and he would be free within five minutes.

One of the pledges had brought along a tube of super glue to play a joke on the smartass senior. As they tied his hands behind his back, the pledge glued the knots together so that they couldn't be untied with anything less than a knife to cut the rope. Then the pledges pulled his pants off and left him there.

Two hours passed before someone thought to check on the senior behind the barn. They were shocked to find that he was almost dead from dehydration. They rushed him to the hospital where the doctors managed to revive him by pumping four quarts of fluids into his veins. As he came out of the coma, his first words were:

"Doesn't that calf have a mother?"

3. This story came from a psychology professor at U.C. Berkeley who said it was his introduction to the sexual revolution that was sweeping the campus in the sixties:

He was assigned to teach the first course in Human Sexual Relationships, which was required for all undergraduates. Finally, the day came for him to give his lecture on the mechanics of the sex act itself between consenting and loving adults. He straightened his tie and approached the blackboard. With a piece of chalk, he wrote down the number 23 on the board and announced: "There are twenty-three basic positions for the act of human sexual intercourse between heterosexual partners."

From the back of the room, a blurry-eyed hippie in a hair shirt with his sandals hanging on his ears cried out: "Twenty-four."

The professor cleared his throat and began again. "There are twenty-three basic positions for the act of human sexual..."

"Twenty-four," came the defiant voice again from the back of the room.

The professor turned around to confront the wiseguy. "OK, we'll count them," he challenged. He turned to the blackboard and began to draw stick figures of a woman on her back and a man covering her from above.

The professor began to narrate: "First, we have the standard prone position with the woman on the bottom and..."

The startled hippie suddenly leaped to his feet and shouted with revelation in his voice: "Twenty-five!"

SCIENCE FOLLIES

1. A scientist friend of mine who worked on the Apollo Man-to-the-Moon project in the sixties told me this story about how the overworked scientists at NASA Huntsville handled the Washington bureaucrats who constantly pestered them for future space flight plans, even though they had not yet completed the Apollo mission. The Huntsville scientists under Dr. Wehrner von Braun cooked up a story about how they had already planned a Man-to-Mars project. One of them would then present their plans to the anxious carpet-baggers from Washington -- complete with elaborate flip charts and cost estimates. The story went as follows:

The most important thing we want to know about Mars is whether there is life on Mars. Does anything reproduce on Mars? So, of course, we sent a reproductive biologist who is best trained to answer this question. He and his able female assistant blast off from earth in a modified Saturn 5 rocket, and 256 days, six hours, and thirty-nine minutes later their space capsule sets down on Mars.

They are immediately greeted by a Martian scientist who looks like a walking hard-boiled egg with one bulging eye and two sensitive antennae swirling about his head.

Our chief scientist asks him how Martians reproduce. The happy Martian takes them into his labortory, pours two test tubes together, and out pops another little egg-shaped Martian. He stands the newborn in the corner and explains that they will educate him later. Then he asks our earthling scientist how human creatures reproduce.

Our scientist and his wide-eyed assistant, in all their exuberance, proceed to demonstrate the human act of sexual intercourse. He then explains to his Martian counterpart that the woman will have another little human being in nine months.

The Martian seems a little confused. He asks, "Why so long?" Our scientist tells him, "That is the gestation period. It takes nine months for the baby to grow inside of her before it comes out."

The Martian's antennae whirl frantically about his head for a moment as he thinks this over, and then he asks: "Well, if you have to wait nine months, why all the hurry there towards the end?"

2.   And who was the world's first computer expert?

It was Eve in the Garden of Eden. She had an Apple in one hand and a Wang in the other.

INVENTORS

1. The story about the Man-To-Mars project prompted another former NASA scientist to call me with his favorite crazy inventor story:

The scene was again Huntsville, Alabama. Governor George Wallace had entered the primaries as a candidate for President. He put out a call to the scientists at Huntsville in which he promised a reward of $50,000 to any inventor who could come up with a way to get rid of the liberal radicals who were heckling him wherever he gave a campaign speech. Eventually, a man appeared at his office one day and said that he had invented a machine that would get rid of radicals. "All you have to do, Governor, is dial in the number you want on this here machine and punch the button. POOF, They're gone ."

The Governor was beside himself. He asked the inventor to come along on a flight to Dallas where the Governor was going to make a speech that afternoon. As they circled over Dallas, the governor pointed down at a crowd that had already assembled to hear his speech. "Mr. Inventor, get me 500 of them radicals down there."

The inventor punched in 500 on his machine and pressed the button. POOF! The ground was vacant where 500 had once stood. They disappeared. The governor was ecstatic. He immediately ordered his pilot to head for Chicago, the site of the Democratic convention in three days.

As the plane circled over Soldiers' Field, they could see the thousands of demonstrators who were already encamped there to demonstrate at the upcoming convention. The Governor ordered the inventor to eliminate 500 of those radicals.

The inventor responded: "Governor, I can only get 499 of them radicals and one politician."

The Governor was taken aback. "What do you mean you can only get 499 more radicals? And why one politician?"

The inventor shrugged and said: "Governor, you got to understand. This here machine is just a prototype. For every 999 of them grubby radicals, we got to grease the machine."

2. Would-be inventors are frequent callers on my talk show because they know I am a scientist by training and hold a few patents. Most want to know a quick way to patent their marvelous ideas. However, almost all amateur inventors are paranoid that someone will steal their invention if they disclose it to anyone.

I give them my standard lecture which says that just the opposite is true. If you don't document your invention (an invention disclosure) and disclose it to witnesses and the patent office, there is no legal way you can ever protect it.

Shortly after I gave this lecture to a caller one night, a fellow called the show to tell me about his uncle who had invented the world's first fold-up and carry-along ironing board for travelers.

His uncle was afraid that someone would steal his idea if he went to a patent attorney, so he decided to take his invention to the U S Patent Office himself. He kept his ironing board hidden under the covers of his upper sleeping berth on the train as he travelled across the country from Los Angeles to Washington, D.C..

By the time the train had reached Kansas, he had struck up a friendship with a lonely lady occupying the upper berth directly across from his. Soon, they were discussing who would move over to the other's berth. But she didn't want the people sleeping below her to see her climbing down from her berth -- and into his.

The resourceful inventor suddenly thought of his folding ironing board. "Say, I have something here long enough to stretch across the aisle and over to your berth and you can crawl over here," he announced.

The wise lady gave him a silly smile and slowly shook her head for a moment. With a deep sigh of disbelief, she answered: "Yes, Romeo. And how do you suppose I'm going to get back?"

3.   Another night, a good-natured fellow called my show to tell me about his first experience as a would-be inventor when he was very young. He spent most of his teen years in his father's shop on the farm in Nebraska building strange gadgets. He said that he found no time for socializing with his peers, in particular, girls. This worried his father to the point that he hitched up the wagon one day and took his son into town.

His father had already located a lady in town who was known to show a man a good time if he came calling with a little money in his pocket. His father made the arrangements and told his son when and where to pick up the lady. He picked her up and sheepishly suggested a ride through the countryside.

He said he struggled to think of something appropriate to say to her, but the only thing he could discuss were his inventions on the farm. It soon became obvious that she was thoroughly bored as they rode along in his horse and buggy. Then mother nature broke the ice for him.

A violent thunderstorm came up and a bolt of lightning hit the horse right between the eyes and killed him deader than a doornail. They sat stone silent for a few minutes in fear. Then, as the storm subsided, he reached over and took her hand. He put her hand on his leg and slowly moved it up to his private parts.

"And what is that?" she asked. But she didn't move her hand away as she popped her bubble gum at him playfully.

Lost for direct words, as usual, he shyly responded: "That's...that's something you put in the right place and it brings life. And it's a lot of fun," he quickly added.

She pursed her lips playfully and nodded thoughtfully over this revelation for a moment. Her hand squeezed his thigh tenderly as she cooed: "Gee, that's nice. So why don't you just stick it up that horse's butt so we can get back to town before dark."

4. A scientist at the Lawrence Livermore National Laboratory called my show to tell this story which he said broke up everyone in the cafeteria one day.

The scientists there traditionally sit at certain tables during noon time to discuss worldly events with their buddies. The topic at his table on this day turned to the world's greatest inventions. A likeable janitor, who was fascinated with science, had joined them at an empty chair with his bag lunch in hand.

One scientist said that alternating-current electricity was certainly the most important invention of man because it was used so widely Another volunteered the transistor as the best, and a third insisted that nuclear energy would prove to be the most valuable. Then the janitor announced:

"Thermos bottle."

The scientists looked around at each other with sly smiles on their faces, but none said a word to embarrass the poor janitor.

As the staff members continued their lively discussion, the janitor insisted again: "Thermos bottle."

To be polite, one of the scientists asked very calmly: "Why do you think the thermos bottle is the most important invention of man?"

The janitor put down his sandwich and responded: "Well, it ain't got no electricity, no transistors, and no nuclear energy. But, still, it keeps hot things hot, and it keeps cold things cold."

The scientists smiled at each other again. One of them snapped at the janitor: "Well, what's so great about that?"

The wise janitor looked very sternly at the dumbfounded scientists and answered:

"But how do it know?"

POLITICIANS

1.   Stevie Smoothy from Iowa was hitchhiking to Hollywood to seek his fortune as a movie star.   In Palm Springs, he got a ride from a man driving an old Cadillac who said he was a part-time actor who now lived in Santa Monica.   Shortly after they were on their way, the dapper old actor asked Stevie which political party he belonged to.   Stevie hesitated before he answered.   He didn't want to lose his ride.   Finally, he decided the guy must be a republican because he owned a Cadillac.

"My family have been republicans for six generations," he blurted out with pride.

The old boy hit the brakes so hard that Stevie almost went into the windshield.   "Get out!" the driver commanded.

Stevie pondered his mistake as he waited more than an hour at a freeway on-ramp for his next ride.   These Californians must all be democrats, and they are sure sensitive about their politics, he concluded.

His next ride was a very pretty young lady dressed in a mini skirt and a tank top and driving an MG sportscar.   They raced down the freeway in her convertible with the breeze blowing in their faces.   Eventually, she too asked him about his political affiliation.   Stevie quickly said he was a democrat this time.   She gave no response.   Stevie was relieved.

Sitting so close to her in the small sportscar, he couldn't help but notice her beautiful body so scantily clad.   Soon, he was fantasizing what she would be like in bed.   As their conversation warmed up, Stevie tried one of his most successful lines with the farm girls back home: "Say lady, you have one beautiful pair of legs there.   I'll bet they sure would feel good wrapped around a man's back in the hay loft."

She pulled to a screeching halt on the side of the freeway and reached across him to open his door as a clear sign that this was the end of the line for him. Shaking her head in disgust, she said: "See, you've only been a democrat for an hour. You got a free ride, and already you're looking around to screw someone."

(I've heard the above joke on the air at election time every year.   The brunt of the joke has been about evenly split between republicans and democrats.   I flipped a coin to pick the party for the punch line this time.   Wouldn't you know it, the democrats came out ahead as usual...)

SKYDIVER

1. Brokenbone Jones had tried about every adventure known to man. Finally, it was time to try skydiving. Typically, he ignored the advice of all to take some lessons first from a licensed instructor. Brokenbone borrowed a parachute and hired a pilot to take him up.

He jumped out at 8,000 feet, sailed through the air with the greatest of ease for several thousand feet -- just like in the movies he had seen -- and finally pulled the rip cord. Nothing happened. Frantically, he searched with both hands for the rip cord to the backup chute, but he couldn't find it.

Then he spotted another man flying up through the clouds below him. As the man passed him, Brokenbone shouted out:

"How do you get this parachute to work?"

The other man looked down at Brokenbone as he soared past him and shouted back:

"Damned if I know -- how do you light a gas oven?"

2. After I stopped laughing long enough to go back on the air, the very next call came from a man who said he had been blind all his life.

"Bill, you know what's the most difficult thing for us blind people who like to skydive?"

"I couldn't even imagine a blind person with the courage to go skydiving," I answered.

"Oh, I enjoy it a lot. It's really no problem at all -- except that it scares the hell out of my dog."

THE WILD WEST

1.   This came to my talk show one night from a cowboy in Arizona:

The Lone Ranger was once captured by the fierce Apache Indians after a great battle. They had him tied up to a post for all to see. The chief came to him and said: "Lone Ranger, you have been a brave warrior. We are going to give you one last wish before we kill you tomorrow."

The Lone Ranger said, "I want to talk to my horse, Silver." So, they cut him loose and he went over and whispered something into Silver's ear. Silver then took off in a gallop and a cloud of dust toward town.

A few hours later, Silver came back leading a wagon train into the Indian's camp.   There were three wagons full of dancehall girls and a wagon full of whiskey. The fierce Apaches had a hell of a party all night.

The next morning, the Chief approached the tied-up Lone Ranger and announced: "Lone Ranger, that was a great party you gave us, but we're still going to have to kill you. However, you can have one more wish."

The Lone Ranger again said, "I want to talk to my horse, Silver."

The chief cut him loose. The Lone Ranger walked over to Silver, slapped his trusty horse alongside the head to get his attention, and then commanded: "Silver, read my lips this time. I said posse, P-O-S-S-E."

2.   A Wyoming cowboy took his faithful cattle dog along with him on a cruise of the South Pacific. The ship sank in a storm and they were the only survivors to wash up on a deserted island once occupied by Australian sheepherders. All that was left were a few sheep.

The cowboy began to fantasize that one of the sheep was his girlfriend back home. He was approaching the ewe with lust in his eyes when his dog barked and scared her away. The next day, the same thing happened. The cowboy decided that his dog was jealous and he would never be able to catch the ewe.

But all his heathen urges vanished a week later when, miraculously, another shipwreck survivor arrived. A beautiful young woman clinging to a piece of driftwood washed up on the beach. She was almost dead from thirst. The cowboy rushed to save her with the last of the precious rain water he had collected for days. She was eternally grateful.

That evening as they lay side by side on the warm beach, she tenderly whispered in his ear, "Is there anything I can do for you -- I mean ANYTHING AT ALL that you want?"

The cowboy thought it over for a minute as he got up on his feet and feasted his eyes on her beautiful, naked body -- from her toes to her nose. Then he sighed, "Well shucks, Mame, I hate to ask you this, seein' your such a nice girl -- but would you mind holdin' on to that damn dog for me for about twenty minutes."

3.   A good ol' boy from Anchorage called to give my audience his story about a famous bear hunter in Alaska who captured his bears alive:

He said that a reporter in San Francisco heard the story and flew to Alaska to interview the hunter. The reporter immediately wanted to see what kind of equipment the hunter used. The proud bear hunter pointed to his little fox terrier, a short piece of rope, and a small .22 caliber pistol in his belt.

"Is that all you use?" asked the reporter in amazement.

"Yup," answered the confident hunter.

"But how do you capture a big bear with just that stuff?" asked the reporter.

The crusty old hunter revealed his secrets: "First, my little dog here chases the bear up a tree. Then I shinnies up the tree and shakes the bear off the limb until he falls to the ground. Then my little fox terrier there runs over and bites him right in the private parts and paralyses him while I gets down and ties him up with this here piece of rope. Nothin' to it."

The reporter looked up from his notebook, somewhat puzzled, and asked: "But why, then, do you carry that little .22 pistol?"

The sly bear hunter spit a slug of tobacco out on the ground, smiled off to the side, and said: "Sonny, that's in case I falls out of the tree first."

4.   A cub reporter for a major metropolitan newpaper was travelling through northern Nevada when he overheard a couple of guys in a coffee shop poking fun at an old cowboy. "How are you and your girlfriend, Suzy the Sheep, getting along these days?" one of them chuckled.

The cowboy jokingly shot back: "At least I ain't broke all the time like you fellers. She comes when I call her and she don't stray away when I'm gone."

The naive reporter was excited that he might have a major story in hand -- a mountain man actually willing to talk about his sexlife with animals. He chased after the cowboy and approached him in a local bar. The wily old cowboy was willing to talk -- so long as the reporter was buying the drinks, of course. He casually described his romantic adventures with Suzy the Sheep while the fascinated reporter furiously took down every gory detail.

As the reporter was paying for the fourth round of drinks for the cowboy and a dozen other old timers at the bar, he thought to ask: "How come a cowboy like you doesn't make love to one of your cows instead of a sheep?"

The cowboy winked at his friends as they lifted the last of their free drinks. Then he drawled matter-of-factly, "Ah, it's just too damn far to go to kiss 'em afterwards."

5. The subject on my show one night focused on the ways that many handicapped people overcame their disabilities and carried on relatively normal lives. Eventually, a good-natured ol'boy from Nevada called to tell his story. He said that he had lost both of his arms in WWII.

One day he decided to visit the local whorehouse in his town. The madam opened the door. She was overwhelmed when she saw a man with no arms at the entrance of her establishment.

"Oh, good Lord," she cried. "I just don't know how you could take care of one of my girls, you poor man."

He replied: "Lady, I rang the doorbell, didn't I ?"

BODY ODOR

1. Three hunting buddies, Jeff, Steve, and Billy Bob, who had known each other since high school were driving to their favorite campsite in northern Nevada in a pickup truck. Jeff and Steve had never had the courage to tell Billy Bob that he had B.O. -- bad. They were driving through the cold night with the windows down, as usual, when a severe thunderstorm forced them to pull into a farmhouse and seek shelter for the night.

The farmer had a spare bedroom, but with only two beds. So he gave them an extra blanket and told them that one of them would have to sleep in the barn. They flipped coins to see who would sleep in the barn. Steve lost. He headed for the barn as the other two took the beds.

About an hour later, there was a knock on the bedroom door. They opened the door to discover Steve with his blanket. "There's a pig out in that barn and the stench is unbearable. One of you will have to go for awhile," he demanded. Jeff and Billy Bob flipped a coin and Jeff lost.

About an hour later, there was another knock on the door. They opened the door to find Jeff. He was back with the same story. "The smell from that pig is unbearable. Billy Bob, it's your turn for awhile." Billy Bob reluctantly took the blanket to the barn.

Sure enough, about an hour later, there was another knock on the door. They opened the door. It was the pig.

2.   Two of Berkeley's finest hippies, Hairshirt and his girlfriend, Moonbeam, were cruising Yosemite National Park in Hairshirt's VW bus when they saw a sign that said: "DO NOT DRIVE OFF THE PAVED ROADS. DON'T HIT THE ANIMALS." Hairshirt immediately turned onto the first unpaved, forbidden road he saw, and they both began to giggle with that special satisfaction

of defying official rules that are made to be broken.

Suddenly, Hairshirt heard a thump under the bus that sounded as if he had hit something. He stopped and stepped out to see what happened. There he discovered a skunk in the middle of the road, still dazed from his collision with the bus. Then Hairshirt saw a green park ranger pickup in the distance, coming up the road behind them.

He grabbed up the dazed skunk by his tail and raced around to the open window by his girlfriend, Moonbeam. "Moonbeam, quick! Hide this animal under your coat. The cops are coming and they'll throw us out of here if they see we hit him."

Moonbeam protested: "But what about the smell?"

Hairshirt shrugged and answered: "Ah, just pinch the little bugger's nose. He'll never know the difference."

LAWYERS

1.   A lady lawyer called my talk show one night when the subject of conversation on the air had turned to discrimination against women in the professions. She told us how one of the most prestigious law firms in town had selected their first woman lawyer from hundreds of applicants. They first reduced the candidate list down to the three best qualified. Then, while each candidate was being interviewed, they slipped $5000 in cash in her briefcase when she wasn't looking. This was to be a test of her integrity.

The first candidate rushed back the next day to return the money that clearly did not belong to her. The second candidate thought it over and invested the money in a hot stock tip that doubled her money in a week. Then she returned the $5000, with interest for a week, explaining that she had discovered the money late because she had gone on vacation. The third candidate thought them all a bunch of old fools and kept the money.

Then my caller said: "Let your talk show listeners guess who got the job."

For the next hour, callers from all over the west coast struggled with this ethical dilemma. Most picked the second candidate because they thought she was both smart and about as honest as any lawyer.

Then the storyteller called back to give us the answer -- and shame us all for our ignorance. "Naturally, they hired the one with the big breasts."

2.   "Bill, I just paid off my ex-wife's lawyer and I learned something. You know what's the difference between a dead skunk and a dead lawyer in the middle of the freeway?"

"Darned if I know," I pleaded.

"There are skid marks leading up to the skunk."

3.   In the middle of a serious discussion on the value of laboratory animals in medical research, a medical student called my talk show to inform the audience that the researchers at his medical school had decided to replace the laboratory rats with lawyers. "Why is that?" I asked.

Calmly he explained, "There are a lot more unemployed lawyers than rats. You can catch all you want by just hanging a bloody dollar bill out the window."   And, with a sigh of professional remorse, he added: "Besides, you can get attached to a rat. And there some things that a rat just won't do..."

4.   What's the difference between a lawyer and a vulture?

Answer: A vulture doesn't take his wingtips off at night.

5.   An angry caller asked me one night: "A lawyer and an IRS agent are drowning. We can only save one of them. What do we do?"

"You got me. What do we do?"

His answer: "Well, do we have a drink or do we go to lunch to celebrate?"

6.   A lawyer walks into his favorite bar with a duck on his shoulder. The bartender asks: "Where did you get that?"

"They're all over the place out there," answered the duck.

7. A recently divorced wife, who said she had taken her lawyer's advice to refuse a reconciliation with her husband, offered this terse comment on my show:

"Bill, what do you call 25 lawyers at the bottom of the bay?"

"Darned if I know."

"A good start."

GOLFERS

1. George was about to tee off on the fifth hole when a funeral procession passed by on the nearby road. George immediately dropped his club, jerked off his golf cap to hold it respectfully over his heart, and bowed his head. After the last car had passed, his partner, Al, said: "George, I never knew you to be so respectful of the dead. Why, we've seen that a dozen times while we were playing this course. You never stopped before."

"I know," George grumbled. "But it's the least I could do. We were married forty years."

2. Forty-year-old Howie and thirty-year-old Suzy decided to get married only ten days after they met in a bar. Howie sat her down for a talk just a few hours before they were scheduled to see the judge.

"Suzy, I have to confess something," he said. "You are probably wondering why I was never married before. I might as well tell you now. I'm a golf addict. I play golf from sunrise to sunset -- every day. And the green fees take every cent I make working at night."

Howie waited anxiously for the rejection he had received so many times before. But he saw only a big smile breaking on Suzy's face. Very cautiously, she said: "Howie dear, I also have something to confess. I'm a hooker."

Howie was stunned in disbelief. But after a few moments to absorb the shock, he put his arms around her tenderly and kissed her cheeks as tears glistened in his eyes. Then he held her at arms length and pronounced sternly: "Dearest one, if you really will marry me, I'll rescue you from that horrible nightmare in a hurry. All we have to do is change your grip on the club little...."

3.   An enterprising young divorcee had just received a handsome settlement check from her third husband. She decided to try golf for the first time in her life. Her lady friends had insisted that she stay behind and take some lessons, but she was sure she could keep up. Sure enough, she sliced her first ball off the tee far into the woods. After ten minutes of searching, she begged her friends to go ahead while she looked for her ball.

Behind some bushes in the forest, she came upon an old man with a long white beard rubbing the sleep out of his eyes as he picked up his backpack from the ground. He held her golf ball in his other hand. As she approached, he spoke:

"Lady, I owe you a debt of gratitude. Your ball hit me and woke me up from a coma that I have been in for ten years. It was a miracle. I must repay you with anything your heart desires. Just tell me your dreams and I'll make them come true."

The lady was fascinated. Good Lord! she thought. He must be Rip van Winkle. She decided to test him.

"I've always dreamed of owning a red Porsche," she said haltingly.

"No problem," said the old man. " When you get home, you'll find it sitting in your driveway."

"Oh my God!" she screamed as she jumped for joy. "Do you think I could also have a mink coat?"

"Most certainly, my dear," the old wizard replied.   "It's hanging in your closet right now."

She danced around in circles at her good fortune. "Oh my God, oh my God," she squealed in disbelief. "You've answered all my dreams. Isn't there something I can do for you?"

The cute old man feigned an embarrassed look on his face and said: "Well, maybe there is. In my coma, I kept hearing these golfers going by talking about something called sex. They made it sound very interesting, but I've never experienced it in my life. Have I missed anything all these years?"

She was overwhelmed with sorrow for this nice old man. Then thoughts of his gratiousness toward her convinced her that she must rescue him. Gently, she instructed the old man in the act of sexual intercourse. And did she get a pleasant surprise! The old boy turned out to be a fantastic lover in the grass.

"Wow," she exclaimed when they were through. "Look what I've been missing all this time. I'm going to take you home with me."

As the sweet old man was buttoning up his pants, he looked down at her and asked: "Lady, how old are you?"

"I'm thirty-three," she answered.

He shook his head in disbelief and asked: "And lady, you still believe in fairy tales?"   (As he took his golf shoes out of his bag...)

4.   Two guys were on the fifth tee when a naked lady came running out of the woods headed straight down the fairway. Next, came a man in a white coat chasing after her. Then a second man in a white coat came along carrying a bucket of sand.

The golfers stopped the second guy and asked what was going on. He explained that the lady was a runaway from the mental institution nearby. She did this almost every day. They were the guards assigned to chase her.

"Yah, said one of the golfers. I can understand the first guy chasing her, but what is this business with the bucket of sand that you're carrying?"

The guard explained: "Oh, I caught her yesterday, so this is my handicap for today."

5.   Sam the Birdiemaster was looking around for a sucker on a slow day at the golf course. An old duffer came in the clubhouse who looked like he might be willing to bet a hundred on a quick nine holes. The old boy said, "Sure, but you'll have to give me three gotch'yas for my handicap."

Sam had never heard this expression for a handicap, but he quickly agreed. Whatever "gotch'yas" might be would make no difference, he thought. This old boy could hardly walk, let alone hit a ball. He 'll be a pushover.

Sam was in his swing on the first tee when the old boy snuck up behind him and goosed him right in the rear with the shaft of a golf club. "Gotch'ya!" shouted the old boy. Sam's first ball landed in the trees.

Two hours later, back at the clubhouse, the bartender saw Sam with a long face counting out a hundred dollars for the old boy. The bartender was incredulous. "Don't tell me that you lost to that old codger?"

Sam shook his head and replied: "You ever try to play nine holes waiting for that next gotch'ya?"

6.   A golfer was carried into the hospital with a horrible gash in his head. The doctor asked him what happened after he came to his senses. The golfer told this story:

He and his wife were on the seventh hole which borders on a cow pasture. His lovely wife had gained a lot of weight and she had decided to take up golf as an exercise. He said he had been joking with her about her belly shaking each time she swung the club, but she was being good natured and laughed along with him.

She sliced the ball on her tee shot and it went into the pasture. He jumped the fence and began looking for it. When he found it, it was lying directly under the tail of a cow that was lying down. He tried to make the cow stand up, but the cow refused to budge.

Soon, his wife came over the fence to retrieve her ball. He said he wanted to be helpful, so he raised the cow's tail and hollared out to his wife: "This looks like yours, Sweetheart."

Still in a state of shock, he told the doctor: "And then for no reason, she just walked up and slugged me with a seven iron."

7.   Harry and Sam were waiting on the sixth hole for two ladies ahead of them to finish up. Harry decided to ask the ladies if he and his partner could play through. He strolled down the fairway to where the ladies were casually chatting while they leaned on their clubs. Fifty feet before he reached them, he suddenly spun around and returned at a fast pace. As he approached Sam, he said:

"Sam, you'd better go over and ask them. I can't. One of them is my wife. The other one is my mistress. It would cost me a mink coat and a new car if they ever ganged up on me together."

Sam chuckled his amusement and started walking toward the ladies. But he too stopped short of them and returned quickly with his cap pulled down over his eyes. "It's a small world, isn't it?"

TEACHERS

1.   An elementary teacher in her third year of teaching brought down the house on my talk show when she gave us this story one night:

Miss Jones, a dedicated fifth-grade teacher and biology major in college, decided that she would introduce her inquisitive class to the basics of human anatomy because it was her opinion that children were gaining a lot of misinformation about human sexuality at an early age. She labored for a month to prepare a special unit on human physiology and then took a full week to present it to her eager students. That Friday, she announced to the class: "Now class, your homework for the weekend is to tell me what part of the human body expands six times when stimulated."

On Monday morning, she pointed to her best student, Melanie, and asked for the answer. Melanie cupped a hand over her mouth to hide her embarrassment and whispered: "My mommy says I can't say it, Teacher."

The teacher then called on little Henry who was wildly waving his hand from the back of the room. "It's the pupil of the eye, Miss Jones."

"Very good, Henry," replied Miss Jones. Then, as she turned to go back to the front of the room, she paused at Melanie's desk and said: "Little girl, I now know three things about you. One, you didn't do your homework. Two, your mommy has a dirty mind. And three, oh boy, when you grow up are you going to be disappointed."

TALK SHOW HOSTS

1.   I got what I deserved one night as I was criticizing greedy lawyers. This caller was probably the very smart wife of one of the dull lawyers I had been arguing with for hours.

She told me the story about an anthropologist from Harvard who was studying a cannibal tribe in the jungle. He entered the local meat market one day to examine how they operated. There he discovered that the special for the day was brains. As he scanned the items on display, he noticed lawyer's brains at $2.00 per pound, scientist's brains for $6.00 per pound, and radio talk show host's brains at the astronomical price of $100.00 per pound!

The anthropologist was incensed that anyone could suggest that the average talk show host was more worthy than a highly trained scientist such as himself. He asked the cannibal butcher: "How come talk show host brains are more expensive than mine?"

The cannibal butcher shrugged his shoulders apologetically and answered: "You know how many talk show hosts it takes to get a pound of brains?"

PROFESSORS

1. A frustrated student from Berkeley called my show to offer this assessment of the faculty. He said that one of his pompous professors was driving to a northern California town one day to give a talk to the local Rotary Club. His trip took him by the state mental institution at Napa. Just as he was passing by, the right front wheel of his car fell off and rolled down the road.

The professor took off his coat, retrieved the wheel, jacked up his car, and then discovered that he couldn't find any of the lug bolts that had fallen out of the wheel. As he cursed the miserable situation he was in, he noticed an inmate from the nut house sitting on the rock wall and smiling, knowingly, in his direction. "Well, wise guy, what would you do?" the annoyed professor demanded, to wipe the smile off this idiot's face.

The inmate calmly answered: "Just take one lug bolt out of each of the other three wheels and use the bolts to put that wheel back on. You'll be OK until you get to a service station and buy some more lug bolts."

The professor was obliged to thank the inmate for saving his day. "Very good, very clever of you, young man," he allowed.

But his station in life demanded that he have the last word, of course. He snidely added: "Fellow, if you're so damn smart, how come you're in the nut house?

The amused inmate shook his head in disgust and answered: "Hey mister, we may be crazy -- but we're not stupid."

2.   A Harvard professor of economics was being driven to a lecture by his trusty chauffeur who had heard his lectures for twenty years. "Professor, what are you going to tell the graduate students today?"

"I think I will give them my lecture on Eastern European economics," said the professor.

"Oh, I've heard that one so many times that I could give the lecture," chuckled the chauffeur.

"You think so, huh? Okay, I'll just let you do that, wiseguy. We'll see if you think its so easy."

He ordered his driver to pull into a service station so they could change clothes before arriving at the university. And, sure enough, the chauffeur delivered the lecture flawlessly while the professor sat quietly in the back of the room. The assembled graduate students applauded respectfully and then began asking questions. The professor, in the chauffeur's cap, smiled to himself. Now, let's see how this smartass high-school graduate does when he has to think on his feet, thought the professor.

The first student asked a long and involved question about what the effect of the end of the cold war would have on the balance of payments between Hungary and the former Soviet states. The chauffeur at the podium listened to the student condescendingly until he had finished his question. The professor thought to himself: now they got him.

The chauffeur began shaking his head disdainfully as he caught the eyes of the audience -- just like his arrogant boss always did to the poor students who dared ask him a question. Then he growled: "Young man, the answer to your silly question is so obvious that even my chauffeur there in the back of the room could answer it."

POLICE

1.   A guy called me one night to tell me how he had gotten out of a speeding ticket. He said he got the cop laughing so hard he couldn't write the ticket, and the cop waved him on.   "This I got to hear," I said.

He revealed his cunning ploy: "I was cruising along at about ninety on the freeway in my new BMW when I saw the CHP patrol car pull out after me," he began. "I just knew he was going to ask me what in the hell I thought I was doing driving so fast. Sure enough, that's the first thing he said.   So I explained to him that just the week before my wife of ten years had run away with a good-looking CHP patrolman."

"He paused for a moment and said he was sorry to hear my bad news, but it didn't explain why I was speeding. So, I told him that when I saw his patrol car behind me, I was afraid he might be trying to bring her back..."

2.   From a beat cop who called my show from San Diego:

A terrified motorist ran into the San Diego police station and asked the desk sargent: "Are there many penguins in San Diego?"

"Many? Are you crazy?" retorted the busy sargent. "There are no penguins in San Diego."

The frantic motorist asked again: "Are you absolutely sure there are no penguins in San Diego?"

The grouchy sargent snapped back: "Hell no I told you. Penguins only live in cold country, mister."

The motorist sighed deep disappointment. Then he asked the sargent: "Officer, are you Catholic?"

The much annoyed sargent ignored him for a moment and then looked up to answer: "As if it's any of your business, mister, I'm Baptist. Now get out of here."

The motorist closed his eyes and slowly volunteered his wrists for the handcuffs.

"What the hell's the problem with you, mister?" barked the sargent.

"I guess I ran over a nun."

3. An argument was raging on my show one night between the hot-rodders and the motorcyclists as to which machines were the fastest. Along came a kid with this cute story that put on end to the argument:

A local high school hot-rodder had built a roadster so fast that every time he stepped on the throttle the car doubled its speed, no matter how fast it was going. He was cruising along the highway one day well above the speed limit. A cop on a motorcycle pulled out after him with the siren wailing. The kid in his hot-rod let the cop catch up, and then he stepped on the throttle and his machine doubled its speed in an instant.

A while later, the ambulance arrived to pick up the badly bruised cop whose motorcycle was scattered in pieces all over the highway. The ambulance driver asked the cop what happened. From the gurney he was lying on, the dazed cop looked up and said: "Damned if I know. I pulled up behind this kid in his hot-rod, and suddenly my motorcycle stopped. So, I got off to see what was wrong with it."

OOPS! I CAN'T BELIEVE I SAID THAT

Quite often, a caller to talk radio presents a situation so outrageous, or makes a statement so absurd, that the host cannot help but try to inject a little humor into the scene to sober the caller. Flippant remarks at these times are often regretted, but it's too late. The words can't be pulled back once they leave the transmitter. Here are a few examples of when I couldn't resist the urge -- and then had to supply station management with lame apologies to irate listeners.

1.   A twenty-three year old woman called my show and asked for advice on what she should do with her aggressive boyfriend. She said, quite convincingly, that she had decided not to have sex before she was married. She wanted my opinion as to whether this was old fashioned. Of course, with a million decent and highly moral people listening, I quickly agreed that she had every right to remain chaste until her marriage. I assumed that she was talking about her future husband.

But then she began a tearful story about all the other frustrated boyfriends she had survived. She claimed she just couldn't understand why none of them had ever invited her to go on trips to romantic places. "All my girlfriends travel all the time with their boyfriends," she cried.

Time was running out on the show. I had to say something profound and complimentary to her to wrap up this conversation because I could imagine the thousands of proper mothers who were listening and thinking of their own proper daughters. "Well, Jane," I interrupted, "in this day and age, you can be proud of your determination. You know what they say. Good girls go to heaven."

And then the irresistable words slipped out of my mouth before my finger could kill the microphone: "And bad girls get to go everywhere else."

2.   A worried young man called me one night to ask if it was bad to not have sex for a long period of time. He said he was well-educated, good looking, and very interested in girls, but that none of his girlfriends seemed to be interested in sex with him. Again, a commercial cluster was coming up and I was racing the clock. With no good advice to offer that I could say on the radio, I thought I should at least humor him a bit until he realized the obvious. So, I told him a story I heard when I was a boy.

I once asked an old logger whether sex was really important for a man's health.   He answered: "Ah, don't worry about it, Willy.   Going without sex for a few years won't hurt your body none.   Why, heck, I went without sex for eleven years once and it didn't hurt me none. And then when I was twelve, this little girl moved in next door..."

3.   A woman called my show with her views on birth control and the population explosion. She quickly had me confused because she was opposed to man-made birth control and, yet, she was certain that high birth rates would ruin the world. No matter how hard I tried, I couldn't get her to see the conflict in her arguments. Then, she blurted out: "Bill, I like sex, but what am I supposed to do to make sure I don't add to the problem?"

In frustration, I answered: "Maria, I guess you'll just have to use an aspirin. It's a good contraceptive, you know."

"How can an aspirin prevent pregnancy?" she asked.

"Just hold it right between your knees -- and don't let go." And then, before I could stop my loose mouth, I chuckled myself into real trouble with: "...and don't bend over in front of strange men."

4.   Another woman called my show to tell me that she had taken my advice to get off welfare. She had applied for a job with the telephone company. She was proud to report that she was now in a training program for operators. She said she was working in Chinatown as an information operator. She was happy as a lark.

The words came out of my flippant mouth before I could stop them: "I'll bet you get a lot of WONG numbers."

(You can bet I got a lot of irate calls from the Chinese community the rest of that night.)

5.   Sometimes a perfectly sincere attempt to answer a caller's question can lead a talk show host into troubled waters. A man was venting his fury on the air one night over his former wife's promiscuous sexual behavior with other men, according to him. Before I could get a word in edgewise, he demanded: "Well, Bill, is she a slut or is she a bitch?"

So, I gave him what I thought he deserved: "Oh, she must be a bitch. You see, a slut is a woman who sleeps with everyone. A bitch sleeps with everyone but you."

PLAY ON WORDS

1.   A librarian teased me with this story one night after I had been showing off with word games I had picked up over the years on radio.   "Dr. Wattenburg," she began very respectfully, "I'll bet you can't guess the answer to this one:

A scientist heard about some amazing dolphins that lived near a south sea island.   These dolphins were reputed to be immortal -- they lived forever.   He set sail to investigate these strange animals.

He asked the natives how he could capture one of these immortal dolphins and they told him the dolphins only came into shore to eat the baby seagulls that fell out of their nests from a cliff high above.

The scientist climbed up the cliff to snatch some of the baby gulls out of their nests to use as bait for the dolphins.   On the top of the cliff, he discovered that the gulls' nests were guarded by a pride of lions.   However, the lions were sleeping in the heat of the day.

The anxious scientist carefully tip-toed over the sleeping lions and gathered up a dozen baby gulls.   But, on the way out, he accidently tripped and woke up the lions.   The lions devoured him on the spot.

Now, you must know why?" she teased.

"I don't get it," I answered.

Then she got me.   "Bill Wattenburg, you should know better. YOU CAN'T TRANSPORT YOUNG GULLS OVER STAID LIONS FOR IMMORTAL PORPOISES."

2. A go-get'em grandmother called my show to give us this one on the air. She had grown tired of listening to a previous righteous lady caller complain about the use of naughty words on the air, such as "hell" and "damn."

Here was her story:

A horny gorilla hid in the bushes until a female bear came down the path. The gorilla grabbed her and attacked her in the bushes. The female bear came out and cried: "Help, help, I'm a lady bruin and I've just been ruined."

By and by came a female ape. The gorilla likewise attacked her. She came out of the bushes crying: "Help, help, I'm a lady ape and I've just been raped."

Next, a poor duck came waddling down the path. The gorilla even grabbed her and pulled her behind the bushes... (I murmured into the microphone, "I think we can guess the rest, grandma," as I reached for the censor button. And then she reminded us all that our dirty minds are the only problem.)

She giggled and closed with: "The duck ran out of the bushes and cried: "Ha, ha, I'm a drake. He made a mistake."

3. A down-and-out hippie told the local preacher that he would do anything for something to eat. The preacher offered him room and board in return for painting the church, but he would have to do it properly. The hippie promised to do the job exactly as instructed, so the preacher gave him enough money to buy ten gallons of paint and thinner and sent him to the paint store.

The hippie stopped along the way to buy a few joints with some of the money the preacher gave him. This left him with only enough money to buy five gallons of paint, but he figured he could dilute the paint with water and no one would know.

He was about finished painting the church when a violent thunderstorm brought torrential rains that began to wash away his water-thinned paint job. The hippie was fearful that the preacher would discover what he had done as he watched the paint run off the wood. "Oh God," he cried. "What will I do now?"

A booming voice came down from the heavens and said: "REPAINT, REPAINT, BUT THIN NO MORE."

4. The owner of a goldmine in 1849 interviewed three men to work in his tunnel, two down-and-out mid-west farmers who had come to California to seek their fortunes, and a Chinese immigrant who had been running a restaurant in San Francisco. The owner decided that the Chinese was the most sophisticated of the three when it came to running a business, so he put him in charge of purchasing and delivering materials to the mine. The other two would work in the tunnel. He gave them their tools, and he told the Chinese that he was in charge of supplies.

A week later, the owner returned to his mine to see how they were doing. He found the two farmers sitting outside the tunnel looking rather nervous and fearful of something. When he asked them what was wrong, they pointed to the tunnel and said: "You go in there and find out."

The owner was making his way along the dark passages of the tunnel when, suddenly, a figure leaped out of the shadows and scared the hell out of him with the scream: "SUPPLIES!"

5. Some callers catch the host completely off guard because their questions sound so serious.

"Dr. Wattenburg, you're a scientist. Maybe you can answer this one for me. How do you make a hormone?"

"Well, that requires knowledge of very complicated chemistry that I couldn't easily explain on the air to a layman..."

"Ah, come on Bill. You just don't pay her."

THE BARROOM

1.   A stranger sat down at the bar and hailed the bartender who was talking to some old-time customers at the other end of the bar.   The bartender brought him his drink and started to walk back to his friends.   The stranger said: "Hey, wait a minute, bartender, I bought a drink. You're supposed to talk to me."

The annoyed bartender returned and said: "Okay, partner. Whatda you want to talk about?"

"I want to talk about atom bombs," annnounced the stranger.

"Atom bombs?" exclaimed the smiling bartender. "OK, but first we'll have to qualify you to talk about a subject that heavy. Let's see now.   You know that rabbits drop little round turds. What do sheep drop?"

Quickly the stranger responded: "Oh, that's easy. They drop little clumps of round turds -- like popcorn balls."

"Very good," said the bartender.   "Now what do elephants drop?"

"Darned if I know," said the stranger, shaking his head.

The proud bartender turned to walk away with a parting comment for all to hear: "See mister, you want to talk about atom bombs -- and you don't know shit."

2.   A late-night caller from Nevada offered this one: A well-dressed city slicker walked into a country bar and ordered a shot of Old Grand Dad. The bartender was out of Old Grand Dad so he poured the cocky stranger a shot of Four Roses, set it on the bar and started to walk away. The stranger took a sip and announced: "Look, I know my liquors. That's Four Roses."

The bartender decided to test the guy. He poured a taste of each whiskey he had behind the bar, one after the other. The stranger correctly named each one. Finally, the bartender gave up and said: "Okay fellow, you can have whatever you want on the house."

The stranger replied: "I'll take the Four Roses."

A shaggy drunk at the end of the bar had been watching the whole scene. He staggered toward the contented stranger and said: "Hey mister, you know your liquors, don't you?"

"Yeh, I know 'em real well," pronounced the stranger.

The drunk reached under his coat and pulled out a small flask. "Here, tell me what this is," he commanded.

The liquor expert took a swig from the flask. He quickly spit it out and snarled: "What the hell! That's piss!"

Smiling through his missing front teeth, the drunk replied: "Yeh, wise guy. But whose?"

3.   A Nevada truck driver on vacation in New York stopped in a local bar in the Bronx to have a beer. He spotted a gorgeous lady looking at him from the other end of the bar. He called the bartender over and told him to send the lady a drink. "And put a little spanish fly in it while you're at it," he added.

The bartender smiled and said: "We don't have no spanish fly. All we got is Macy's fly."

The truck driver had never heard of Macy's fly, but he didn't want to sound stupid, so he just shrugged and said: "Fine. That'll do."

The bartender delivered the drink to the lady. She beamed her appreciation to the truck driver as she took a taste of the free drink. He watched her intently out of the corner of his eye as her head jerked back and her eyes widened with instant exhilaration.

She gulped down the drink, checked her makeup, and began walking toward him. The truck driver winked at the bartender with anticipation. The bartender whispered:

"Hey, just brace yourself, fellow. We know how to handle these dames here in New York."

The suddenly amorous lady threw her arm around the truck driver from Nevada, pecked him on the cheek tenderly, tickled his ear with her tongue, and said: "Want to go shopping, big boy."

SENIOR SEX

1. Dapper Dan from Hollywood and Miss Julie from Nashville, both in their late seventies, were residents of a retirement home in Arizona. One evening, old Dan put on his best suit, bought a bottle of wine, and went courting Julie in her downstairs apartment. She was quite taken with his romantic overtures, and they ended up in bed.

She woke him early the next morning to remind him that he had better go back to his room upstairs before the nurse arrived with his medication. As he left, he sheepishly handed Julie a ten dollar bill. She was a bit confused by this, but he was gone before she could ask why.

Dan approached her that afternoon at the lunch table. Her lover of the night before immediately struggled to explain his strange behavior:

"Julie dear, I wanted desperately to give you a token of my appreciation this morning. The ten dollars was the only thing I had to offer for the great compliment you paid me last night. I didn't know you were a virgin. What a wonderful thing that you saved yourself all these years just for me."

Dainty Julie almost choked on her sandwich as she broke into giggles. She discreetly checked over her shoulder to see which nosey residents might be listening, and then whispered to Dapper Dan as he basked in his glory:
"Deary, if I had thought that you could still get it up, I would have taken off my panty hose."

2. Ma and Pa, in their late sixties, were experiencing a dramatic slowdown in their formerly healthy, if not frequent sex life. Ma suggested that they both go in for medical examinations. Pa reluctantly agreed, and Ma quickly set up the appointment.

Pa was a bit annoyed and not at all cooperative when the doctor examined him, so the doctor met with Ma in his office and told her: "We'll need a stool sample, a urine sample, and a semen sample from Pa. Do you think you can get him to go along with that?"

"No problem," said Ma.

As she walked out into the waiting room, Pa growled at her and demanded: "What does he want now?"

"Pa, he says you leave your shorts here."

3.   Farmer Jones, sixty-five, went to the urologist complaining that he was unable to father a child with his new wife. The nurse told him that the doctor would need a semen sample before his examination. She gave him the sample bottle and showed him to the men's room, leaving the rest up to his imagination.

An hour later, she was knocking on the door to see why he hadn't delivered a sample. Shortly, Farmer Jones came out and announced:

"Mame, I've tried everything. First, I used my right hand. Then I used my left hand. Then I used both hands. And, finally, I even banged it on the wall. But no matter what I do, I can't get the lid off that damn little bottle.

RIDDLES

THE MISSING DOLLAR (THREE MEN IN A HOTEL)

The case of the missing dollar is probably the most often recited riddle I've heard from the general audience in the past twenty years on talk radio. The answer to this riddle just doesn't make sense to the common man -- and it's equally difficult to explain to most who take simple arithmetic for granted. In fact, the explanation I offer has sometimes generated enough frustration for disbelieving callers that they are tempted to jab me a bit for being a smartass, as you will see in the story that follows this one.

The "Three Men in a Hotel" riddle goes as follows:

Three men enter a hotel and pay ten dollars each for a room. `After they leave, the clerk discovers that he should have charged them only twenty-five dollars total. The clerk gives the bellman five dollars to return to the men. The bellman doesn't know how to split five dollars three ways, so he gives each of the men back only one dollar and he keeps two dollars.

Now, each man has paid only nine dollars out of pocket, right? Three times nine is twenty-seven plus the two dollars in the bellman's pocket equals twenty-nine. Where did the other dollar go?

The frustrating (for most people) answer to this seeming paradox is that the above calculation makes no sense because it is adding apples and oranges. The calculation says nothing more than "twenty-seven plus two equals twenty-nine." The listener is made to think that it should add up to thirty because the question is asked and thirty was the initial amount paid.

The net twenty-seven dollars paid by the men is relevant only when you try to account for where it went, that is, twenty-five to the clerk and two to the bellman. Adding the bellman's two to the twenty-seven and expecting it to equal another number such as thirty is simply nonsense.

The rules of arithmetic guarantee only that the sum of the parts will equal the whole. The calculation used in this riddle does not add up the proper parts to equal the proper actual amount paid out by the men, any way you want to look at it. This is the kind of fast shuffle used by con men to cheat unsuspecting cashiers.

If you want to say that thirty dollars was paid out in the beginning, you can add up the appropriate parts to equal the whole as well: twenty-five to the clerk, two to the bellman, and three back to the men equal thirty

This seems like a paradox to many people (and slow cashiers who end up short at the end of the day) only because someone makes them focus on the wrong total (thirty dollars) while they are being led through a meaningless calculation such as the one in this riddle.

The lesson is that you must understand the rules of arithmetic before you trust any calculation, particularly someone else's calculation.

GIVE THE POSTMAN A DOLLAR

The above explantion to the Three-Men-In-A-Hotel riddle, which I've attempted to give dozens of times on the air, is still unsettling to many. One very agitated woman argued with me for twenty minutes on the air. "But where did the other dollar go?" she kept insisting. I kept giving her the same answer. There is no other answer.

With a final sigh of frustration she said: "Bill Wattenburg, I have another riddle for you. And this one will tell you what I think of your explanation for the missing dollar." I was delighted she wanted to change the subject.

"My best girlfriend has been married for fifteen years to a grouchy husband who never talks to her. All he ever does is come home, plop down in front of the television, open a beer, and grunt if she asks him a question.

Well, on Christmas Eve day, she opened the door to meet the postman. She was wearing only her sexiest underwear. She invited him in and then seduced him on the couch. Then she reached in her purse and gave him that missing dollar we have been arguing about. And then, before the poor, dumbfounded postman could say a word, she shoved him out the door. Now, you tell me why?"

I could find no rhyme or logic to this story, so I stuck my chin out. "Alright, tell me the answer."

"Why, it's as easy as your arithmetic explanations to me, Bill," she continued. "The poor housewife had this grouchy husband who never talked to her. He never explained anything to her in a way she could understand. He just grunted some dumb answer whenever she asked a question. OK?

So she asked him the night before: 'What should we give the postman for Christmas?'

Obviously, he just brushed her off and grunted: 'Ah fuck the postman --- give him a dollar.'"

The engineer, producer, and I all had access to a censor button. Not one of us could pick ourselves off the floor quick enough to hit it within the four seconds required. Her words sailed out over the airways to the West Coast. And would you believe that there was only one protest letter. Even this lady said simply: "I couldn't believe my ears.   Vulgar, but maybe appropriate."

But oh, did I smart for awhile over that one. There isn't a month that goes by that I don't meet some woman somewhere who heard the story on my show that night. When this typically very proper lady sees me, she checks over her shoulder that no one is listening, cracks a big smile, jabs her finger at me like a toy pistol, and giggles: "Ah screw him. Give him a dollar."

THE TRUTH TELLERS AND LIARS

The second most popular category of riddles I've been asked to explain are the truth-teller/liar problems. A simple one goes as follows:

There are only two tribes in the jungle. One, the Truth-tellers who always tell the truth without fail, and, two, the Liars who aways lie. That is, they always say the opposite of what they know to be the truth.

A scientist is seeking the Truth-tellers tribe. He comes to a fork in the road. He knows that one way leads to the Truth-tellers, the other way to the Liars. There is a native standing at the intersection. The scientist does not know whether the native is a Truth-teller or a Liar.

The problem is: What one question can the scientist ask the native such that the answer will tell the scientist the way to the Truth-tellers tribe, no matter whether the native is a Truth-teller or a Liar?

There is a very simple solution, but it is not obvious unless you have some guiding principles to find it. I try to make those who ask for a solution on radio think about these principles a bit before I give them an answer. This too has led to some choice blasts of frustration from listeners who didn't want their minds taxed. "Just the answer, damnit!"

The first principle says that the question asked must bring the same answer from either a Truth-teller or a Liar. If the two would answer differently, the scientist would not know which answer to trust. And he can't ask a second question.

The second step is to realize that the value of any trial question can be tested by simply trying it on a Truth-teller and then a Liar. If you get different answers, it won't solve the problem. With these rules in mind, I'll give you an answer and then show how the rules led to it, for me at least.

All the scientist has to do is ask the native: "Which way is your tribe?" Let's test it to see if we get the same answer, independent of who the native might be, Truth-teller or Liar.

A Truth-teller will point to his tribe -- because he knows it is the truth and he always tells the truth. A Liar knows the direction to his tribe. But he aways lies, so he will point in the opposite direction. He also points to the Truth-teller's tribe. So, both will point to the Truth-teller's tribe.

The scientist does not have to worry about who the native is. He has his answer, the direction to the Truth-teller's tribe. The problem is solved with this simple question.

And by the time I get through with this elaborate explanation, I've lost most of my audience. There are other more complicated questions that could be asked to solve the problem, but they require even more elaborate explanations to prove that they are valid solutions.

Interestingly, we all encounter many situations in life where we do not trust the source of information that is being given to us, that is, we're not sure we are dealing with a truth-teller. Consequently, we invent many ways to extract valid information from an unreliable source, often times unconsciously. The truth-teller, liar riddle is instructive in that it makes us realize that this sometimes can be done in a very logical way.

THE TWO COMPUTERS PROBLEM

Another popular version of the truth-teller/liar riddles comes in a more complicated form:

There are two computers in a closed room. One computer always tells the truth, the other always lies. You don't know which is the liar, but each computer knows what the other one is.

There are only two doors out of the room. One door leads to certain death, the other door leads to freedom. You are trapped in the room. You may ask one and only one question of either computer, but not both, to find the door to freedom. What question can you ask one computer such that the answer will tell you the door to freedom with absolute certainty? Remember, you don't know whether you are addressing a liar or a truth-teller.

The same principles, or rules, as above still apply. However, you have to think ahead a little more to formulate a question that cancels out the uncertainty of which computer you are talking to. And, this time, the computers are not associated with the directions, the doors, as was the case with the natives above who belonged to one of the tribes.

One solution is to look at either computer and ask it the question: "If you ask the other computer which way is the door to freedom, what will it say?"

Again, let's test the validity of the solution with the first rule: do we get the same answer independent of the computer we address?

Assume we ask the truth-telling computer (without knowing it). The truth-telling computer knows the other computer is a liar. When the truth-telling computer asks the liar to point to the door to freedom, the liar will point to the door to death. The truth-telling computer will answer the original question put to it by correctly saying that the other computer, the liar, pointed, to the door to death.

When the question is put to the liar computer, it knows that the other computer will truthfully point to the door to feedom. The liar computer will lie and say that the other computer pointed to the door to death.

Hence, once again, both answers are the same. By asking the above question, you know for sure that either computer will point to the door to death, no matter which one you address with the question. Now, all we have to assume is that you don't want to die and you will be smart enough to go out the opposite door, the door to freedom.

FOX, CHICKEN, AND CORN

This riddle, often recited by frustrated callers, is one that has appeared in many puzzle books and other publications over the years. It goes as follows:

A man owns a fox, a chicken, and a bag of corn. He must keep them separated. Otherwise, the fox will eat the chicken, or the chicken will eat the corn. He can only keep them separated when he is near them.

He must move all three across a river in a small rowboat. The boat will only hold him and one of the three items during each passage across the river. How does he get them all to the other side, one at time, without the fox eating the chicken or the chicken eating the corn when he is not present?

Clearly, he has to make at least three trips, and he must take the chicken on the first trip. If he takes the fox first, the chicken will eat the corn while he is gone. If he takes the corn first, the fox will eat the chicken while he is gone.

So, he takes the chicken to the opposite shore first. But, now, which one does he bring over on the next trip? If he brings the fox to the opposite shore, the fox will eat the chicken there while he goes back for the corn. If he brings the corn next, the chicken will eat the corn while he goes back for the fox. Here is the dilemma.

Obviously, he must do something other than bring them across one at a time. When you think about it, the only thing that he can possibly do is to take something back with him on the boat on the return trips. Here lies the solution.

He must take the chicken across on the first trip, as explained above. Then he returns to bring the fox over on the second trip. Then he realizes that he cannot leave them together on the opposite shore, so he does the only thing he can. He takes the chicken back with him in the boat on the second return trip. He leaves the chicken back where it started and takes the corn over on the third trip. Now, only the fox and corn are together on the opposite shore while he goes back and brings the chicken over on the fourth and last trip. At no time are the fox and chicken together or the chicken and corn together when he is not present. Thus, his problem is solved.

Note that he could have taken the corn over on the second trip instead of the fox. He still would have to do the same thing, that is, take the chicken back and then bring the fox over.

The critical insight here is that he must keep the chicken separated from the other two, or with him at all times, to prevent either the chicken or the corn from being eaten when he is not present.

BOY IN THE ELEVATOR

A very bright kid stuck me with this riddle:

A delivery boy carrying a heavy package entered the elevator of a skyscaper and punched the button to the twenty-first floor. He got out and walked the stairs all the way up to the forty-fifth floor. Exhausted, he finally delivered the package. Then he went back to the elevator, punched a button, and came out at the ground floor. Why did he walk the top twenty-four floors and, yet, ride all the way down?

I made three different guesses, all wrong.

This third-grader must have been saying "shame on you for being so ignorant about the problems little kids face," when he gave me the answer:

"The delivery boy was too short to reach above the button for the twenty-first floor on the elevator panel."

ELEPHANTS IN THE HOLE

One bright kid on the air always attracts another. I think their parents must wake them up to prove that their kid is smarter than the one they just heard. A sixth-grader called with this riddle a few minutes after the elevator riddle above:

A scientist discovered a herd of elephants trapped in a deep canyon in Africa. There was no way they could climb out. The scientist thought and thought, but he could think of no easy way to get them out without using very expensive helicopters. Then his daughter had a bright idea.

She told her father to have his native helpers take a dozen fruit jars down to the elephants. Then, from the cliff above, she just turned his binoculars around and the natives put the elephants in the fruit jars and carried them out.

WHAT DO MEN DO AFTER SEX?

A lady who identified herself as a sociologist studying human sexual behavior called one night to give my audience this straight-faced report:

She had just published a scientific paper in a psychology journal on the results of her study of what men do after sex. In summary, she said, fifty-two percent go to sleep, eighteen percent read a book until they fall asleep, and twenty percent watch TV or listen to the radio. I immediately pointed out that her numbers didn't add up to 100 percent.

"What do the other ten percent do?" I asked, just as she expected.

"Oh, they just go home," she giggled.

THE SURGEON'S SON

A favorite of the little kids who stick me with riddles has always been this one:

A man and his son are riding in a car. They are struck by another car. The man is killed. The son is taken to the hospital seriously injured. There, the tall surgeon on duty takes one look at the boy and exclaims: "I can't operate on this boy. He's my son."

"How could this be?" asked the caller.

The answer escaped me the first time I heard it.

The little girl on the telephone chided me:

"See, if you weren't such a male chauvinist, you would realize that the surgeon has to be the boy's mother."

HOW OLD ARE THE CHILDREN?

This is one of the most bothersome puzzles ever given to me on the air. At first, it seems impossible to solve with only the clues that are offered. I foolishly said this to the caller who hit me with the problem. A few minutes later, I looked at it again during a commercial break and scolded myself for not putting my brain in gear before opening my mouth. Here is the puzzle:

A census taker rings a doorbell and asks the homeowner for the ages of his three children. The father says: "The sum of their ages is equal to my house number."

The census taker answers: "That's not enough information."

The father then says: "Well, here's another clue. If you multiply their ages together, the product is 36."

The census taker says: "That's still not enough information."

The father says: "OK. I'll give you one more clue. My one oldest child plays the piano."

The census taker thinks for a moment, thanks the father, and writes down the correct ages of the three children. How did he figure out the ages of the children with just the three clues given above?

At first, the statement that their ages add up to the father's house number seems to be meaningless because we don't know what the number is. The problem begins to unfold when you realize, however, that the census taker knows the number. He's looking at it. And he is the one that counts. We've been asked to explain how he solved the problem. In the course of figuring that out, we can also find the answer.

So, the census taker knows the sum of the three ages because he can read the house number. And, he quickly realizes that there are only a few combinations of three numbers that have a product equal to 36 -- eight to be exact. They are:

$$(1,1,36) \quad \text{sum}=38$$
$$(1,2,18) \quad \text{sum}=21$$
$$(1,3,12) \quad \text{sum}=16$$
$$(1,4,9) \quad \text{sum}=14$$
$$(1,6,6) \quad \text{sum}=13$$
$$(2,2,9) \quad \text{sum}=13$$
$$(2,3,6) \quad \text{sum}=11$$
$$(3,4,3) \quad \text{sum}=10$$

Now, if you look at the above possible combinations of the three ages, you'll notice that the sum of each group is different (unique), except for 1,6,6 and 2,2,9 which both add up to 13. If the house number matched one of the groups that has a unique sum, the census taker would know immediately that it was the answer, and the only possible answer. He would not have needed the third clue.

The reason he needed the third clue has to be because the house number is 13 and there are two possible answers (1,6,6 and 2,2,9) which add up to 13. He can't determine which of these two combinations is the answer without more information.

Now we see the significance of the last clue: "My **one** oldest child..."

If there is only one oldest child, the ages of the children cannot be 1,6,6. The clever census taker now knows that the correct ages of the children must be 2,2,9.

But just try explaining this on the air in two minutes sometime. Believe me, you will lose a lot of friends -- until you write it down and send a copy to each and every one of them so they can think it over for awhile. I imagine that the caller who first gave me the problem knew this would happen to me if I dared to solve it on the air.

THIRTEEN CARDS IN ORDER

This is my very favorite over the years. This card trick puzzle has convinced many people, young and old, that they are a lot smarter than they thought they were. It's a great party game. You need only a deck of playing cards. The solution requires no particular training or background. In fact, bright kids often solve it quicker than a Ph.D. in physics.

To understand the objective of the puzzle, you first need to practice the following simple exercise. Take the thirteen cards of any suit from the deck, say, all the spades. Hold this deck of thirteen cards face down in your hand. Now, here is the way you will deal out the cards face up on the table:

Deal the top card face up. Slide the next card in your hand, face down, back under the deck. Deal the next card face up on the table. Slide the next card in your hand back under the deck, and so on. In other words, **deal every other card face up on the table with the intermediate cards going back under the deck in your hand, face down.** Do this until there is only one card face down left in your hand. Finally, deal it face up on the table.

Now, here is the objective. We want the sequential order of the cards that you deal face up on the table to be ace, two, three.....up to the king, in that order. The question is: **What should be the original order of the cards in your hand face down such that when you deal every other one out on the table by the above procedure you will get a sequence on the table which is ace, two, three...up to the king?**

It looks easy, and it is -- in the beginning. But just try it. You will learn a lot about logical thinking before you solve this one. Almost anyone will solve it sooner or later by trial and error. Study what you are doing as you find a solution and you will see some simple rules. Now, study the rules you've discovered to see why they work. Remember these rules for the next time you try this puzzle. Otherwise, I guarantee you that you will be embarrassed when you proudly challenge someone else with this puzzle and then discover that you can't solve it the first time you deal out the thirteen cards!

When you discover the rules, however, you can easily change the objective to anything you'd like and solve the puzzle for this new objective. For instance, change the objective to be king, queen, jack, ten .... down to the ace for the order of the cards dealt out on the table. This is the inverse order. No problem -- if you discovered the simple logical rules that you must follow to order the cards in your hand in the beginning.

This puzzle is probably the very best and most simple test I've ever found for native intelligence and the ability to focus on a problem. Many times I've encountered children who were thought to be slow or "not too bright." But once they decided that playing with the cards was a fun game and they focused on the objective, many of them not only quickly solved the problem but they also discovered the rules that lead to a solution---and they remembered these rules when I gave them a different form of the puzzle! Pick any four people and give each of them one of the four suits from a deck of cards. Give them this puzzle. You'll get a surprise. Most often the first to solve the puzzle is not the one you thought to be the most intelligent.

THE SPINNING QUARTER ON THE BAR

Some radio fans always seem to find a way to put me in my place, even when I'm off the air.

I stopped in my favorite bar after my radio show one night to be greeted by a grubby guy in cowboy hat and boots sitting at the bar. As I passed by, he commented: "You were showing off tonight."

I smiled sheepishly and walked on rather than get engaged with a gushing radio fan off the air. At any rate, he was already demonstrating something to the curious bartender. I took a stool far down the bar to avoid his attention.

Soon, my curiosity forced me to peek at his strange behavior. He was spinning a quarter on the bar and touching it with the flame of a lighted match. Each time he tried it, he mumbled to the bartender, "it's not going to work on this wooden surface."

But, still, he kept lighting matches and spinning the quarter. I searched my mind for what kind of scientific phenomonen he was trying to demonstrate. Was it a vortex effect? Would the air around the spinning quarter suck the flame of the match upward into a spiral? No, he couldn't possibly spin the quarter fast enough to accomplish that, I concluded.

Could the flame wrap entirely around the spinning quarter if he spun it fast enough? And the flame was close enough? Maybe that was it? I hid my face behind my upraised drink to conceal the fact that I was eavesdropping.

I closed my eyes to make a quick mental calculation while pretending total disinterest. No, I concluded. Simple physics said that the heat of the flame would cause the air to expand and rise upward before the air current generated by the spinning coin could pull the flame in a horizontal direction around the quarter.

Ten minutes later, he was still spinning the coin, following it with the flame of another match, and complaining to the stoic bartender that his trick just wasn't going to work tonight. Surely, I thought, this guy was trying to demonstrate some profound scientific phenomonen that was simply impossible. I could stand it no longer. I had to save him from his scientific ignorance.

"Mister, if you're trying to do what I think you are, there's a little basic physics that you should understand," I said politely.

A big smile broke on his face. The bartender grimiced and moaned his disappointment. The grubby stranger held the quarter up for me to see, with the eagle side of the coin facing me. He pointed to the bird stamped on the coin. "No physics necessary, Doc. I'm just trying to burn the tailfeathers off this eagle's ass."

The faithful bartender had bragged for years to his customers that his favorite talk show host could figure out anything. He shook his head at me, sighed, and turned to the cash register. He ripped out a twenty-dollar bill and reluctantly paid off the bet he had obviously made with this smirking gunslinger who had waited so patiently in ambush to beat me at the draw.

The seemingly ignorant stranger at the bar was wise enough to know that busybody curiosity will always trap an over-educated smartass who can't keep his nose out of other people's business -- and keep his damn mouth shut when it's none of his business.